The Church's 'Public Service'

Edited by Bryan Cones

Australian Journal of Liturgy
Volume 19 Number 4 (2025)

Council 2025

President:	John Francis Fitz-Herbert, BTh, GradDipMin, MThStud (Liturgy), CPS
Deputy President:	Kieran Crichton, BMus, MMus, MDiv, PhD
Journal Editor:	Bryan Cones, BA, MA, GradDipTheol, PhD
Secretary:	Jennifer Close, BA Fine Arts, Dip Ed, GradDipTheol, PhD

Chapter Convenors:

Queensland	Francis Fitz-Herbert, BTh, GradDipMin, MThStud (Liturgy), CPS
New South Wales	David Nelson, BAppSc, GradDip UrbReg Planning, MBS, MTheol
Victoria	Kieran Crichton, BMus, MMus, MDiv, PhD
South Australia	Alison Whish, BA BSocAdmin, BTh, MTh, Dip Min
Western Australia	Angela McCarthy, BA, BEd, MEd (RE), MTheol, PhD

Membership of the Academy

Admission to the Academy is open to those who have recognised qualifications in liturgical studies and related disciplines. The Academy also admits those who have demonstrated in other ways their professional competence in these fields or who evidence a developing contribution in the area of worship. The Academy hopes that the work of members will serve to animate the liturgical spirit of the traditions and congregations to which they belong.

Applications are invited and should be made on an application form available from:

Australian Academy of Liturgy
The Secretary
c/o Dr Jenny Close
liturgy.australia@gmail.com

The Church's 'Public Service'

Complicated, Complex, or Chaotic?

Edited by Bryan Cones

Adelaide
2025

Australian Journal of Liturgy
Volume 19 Number 4 2025

Copyright © Australian Academy of Liturgy

ISBN
978-1-923603-81-3   Soft
978-1-923603-82-0   Hard
978-1-923603-83-7   Epub
978-1-923603-84-4   PDF

Australian Journal of Liturgy

VOLUME 19 **NUMBER** 4   2025

Editor	Bryan Cones, BA, MA, GradDipTheo, PhD
Associate Editor	Angela McCarthy, BA, BEd, MEd (RE), MTheol, PhD
Book Review Editor	Michelle Eastwood, BA, GDE (Sec), MEd, MA, PhD
Editorial Panel	Angela McCarthy, BA, BEd, MEd (RE), MTheol, PhD
	Marian Free, DipEd
	Jason McFarland, BMus (hons), MMus, MA, PhD, SFHEA
	Barry M Craig, SLD
	Clare Schwantes, BA (Psych), BEd, DipEditPub, MTheolSt (Liturgy), PhD, GAICD
	Adam Couchman, BTh (hons), MA, PhD

AJL is the journal of the Australian Academy of Liturgy and exists to further the study of liturgy at a scholarly level, and to comment on and provide information concerning liturgical matters with special reference to Australia. AJL is published twice a year.

ISSN 1030-617X

Cover: Australian Academy of Liturgy 2025 Conference Image
Art: Jenny Close

Design and Production: ATF Press

Published by:

Making a lasting impact
An imprint of the ATF Press Publishing Group
owned by ATF (Australia) Ltd.
PO Box 234
Brompton, SA 5007
Australia
ABN 90 116 359 963
www.atfpress.com

Contents

Editorial   1

Articles

* Radical Welcome and Texts of Terror: Attending to the Complexities of Liturgical Practice   5
    Peter Catt

* 'The Congregation Is Not an Audience': Expanding the Meaning of Participation in Worship   25
    Matthew Julius

* Eucharistic Concelebration Within a Synodal Church: What Appropriate Today?   39
    Paul Taylor

* Clanging Symbols: Gender and Ordination in the Lutheran Church of Australia and New Zealand   55
    Michelle Eastwood

* Glory and Justice in Christian Living and Worship   71
    Jenny Close

Articles with an asterisk (*) are peer reviewed.

Academy Reports
From the President   83
From the Chapters   84

Book Reviews

What is Happening to Religion in Australia? Understanding the Trends
    by Philip Hughes   89
    Reviewed by Stephen Burns, Victoria

Mystery Manifest: The Triune God, Figuratively Speaking
    by Gail Ramshaw   93
    Reviewed by Annie Brophy, Victoria

AJL Addresses   97

Editorial

The topic of the Academy's conference in January 2025, liturgy and justice—featuring Gerard Moore's trenchant query, 'Why is this still a question?'—has achieved a new urgency for many Christians in my United States (US) context, with so much injustice, especially against new arrivals to the country, on grotesque display. What gets less coverage, perhaps, is the liturgical forms of resistance cropping up. At a US Immigration and Customs Enforcement (ICE) 'processing facility' in Broadview, Illinois, outside Chicago, Fridays and Saturdays have featured interreligious and First Nations prayer gatherings, interdenominational eucharist and Roman Catholic eucharistic processions, Unitarian 'flower communion', Bible studies and hymn sings—nearly the entire cornucopia of 'liturgy' broadly understood deployed in the hopes of turning the hearts of perpetrators or sustaining those detained. To some eyes, mine included, it is the definition of *leitourgia,* public service gesturing toward the borderless divine commonwealth. To some of my other religious siblings, Christians among them, it is the politicisation, even weaponisation, of the biblical and liturgical heritage. Who is right? It is complicated, and it has direct impact on how these issues filter into the Sunday-by-Sunday prayer of many churches.

'Complicated' is indeed a word for our times, and not just in the US, and the churches' responses in common prayer and liturgy to our complex contexts are no less so. Peter Catt's keynote from our January conference, which opens this issue, invokes the Cynefin Framework, with its Simple, Complicated, Complex, and Chaotic taxonomy of systems, to chart the effects of change in liturgy. Unintended consequences loom large in the interaction of the received liturgical heritage, the history of its use, and the personal and communal stories that interact in any liturgy. Tugging at one string may well disrupt more than one other in such a complex system. How can assemblies shape liturgies that gesture toward justice now while still maintaining strong roots in what has been received, however problematic?

Matthew Julius' contribution turns attention to the celebrating assembly—'not an audience'—and the 'publics' it presumes and addresses. While the language of 'participation' is endemic to conversation about good liturgy, the questions of who participates, and how, and for what purpose are often left insufficiently answered. Julius' attention to 'publics' and 'counter-publics', active and passive participation, and ambiguity suggest an assembly with porous boundaries, one able to engage and address the presence of Christ in the world.

Paul Taylor's contribution on the Roman Catholic practice of concelebration in a Synodal Church at first glance turns inward to a particular denominational liturgical practice, though one that reflects how churches organise themselves in service to the world. Does a wall of vested presbyters lined up in front at diocesan celebrations suggest a church in which all the baptised are full participants? Taylor's reflections on the dangers of a liturgically warranted two-tiered church found a similar expression in last July's meeting of *Societas Liturgica:* At the final eucharist, some two dozen Roman Catholic priests vested and concelebrated in the chancel near the altar, while the broadly ecumenical assembly gathered in the nave. While the division enacted was perhaps unintentional, it provided a 'ritual picture' that might also benefit from Taylor's good questions. Michelle Eastwood's reflections on the 'clanging symbol' of gender in relation to ordination among Australian Lutherans adds further dimension to the ways ordination and liturgical leadership inscribe hierarchy in assemblies.

Jennifer Close's reflections on the intersection of justice and glory as mediated through liturgy direct readers to a difficult reality: While we may hope to gesture toward and praise God's 'glory' in common prayer, that glory is in no way reflected 'on earth as in heaven'. Invoking John's gospel, Close reminds us that divine glory—not least in John's 'glorified Christ'—does not at all reflect the kinds of 'glory' human societies celebrate. It is complicated to say the least. Two book reviews on complicated topics round out this issue, the first on the complicated religious landscape, and the second on the complex challenges of naming God in assemblies. There is nothing 'simple' about any of it.

This issue also collects some of the last of the contributions shared at our January conference—though the intersection of liturgy and justice is hardly exhausted. As we look forward to the next volume of the journal, and especially its next issue, we will point again toward liturgical celebration in the contexts of Australia, New Zealand, and the Pacific. How would you like to contribute?

Radical Welcome and Texts of Terror: Attending to the Complexities of Liturgical Practice

Peter Catt

Peter Catt holds a BD and a PhD in evolutionary microbiology and is Dean of St John's Anglican Cathedral, Brisbane. His interests include Christian formation, the science and religion dialogue, and narrative theology. Peter understands justice to be a core spiritual value. He serves on Anglican and Ecumenical Social Justice Committees at a diocesan and national level.

Abstract

As we become increasingly aware of the complexity of the world and the web of human relations, and how that complexity impacts on our desire to see God's commonwealth emerge on Earth, we would do well to heed the call issued at the beginning of the divine liturgy 'to attend'.

What Is Liturgy for Anyway?

My 'conversion experiences'—what for me were experiences of having my being affirmed, discovering deep acceptance and feeling a profound and abiding sense of being loved and having a purpose— did not take place in a church or in any other religious context. (I call them 'conversion experiences' to adopt the terminology used by many in the church, even as I begin to address the complexity of religious experience that is so often ignored by the asker of the question, 'When did you become a Christian?') Rather they happened in the natural environment, starting at a time when I hardly had language at all and continuing into the times when, despite having the gift of language, I had no words to describe what I was experiencing.

Everything gelled for me when, late one evening, I was drawn into a small church building by the singing of a small group of people. Knowing what I know now, I am pretty sure that I had stumbled on what in those days was an 'illegal' Tridentine Mass. I did not understand a word of what was being said, but the look of delight on the faces of those who were involved in that act of worship, combined with the beautiful simplicity of the music that they were making with voices alone—a form of plainsong, I guess—reminded me of the experiences I had had at the beach and in the bush.

The closest I have come to finding words that honour my experiences at the beach, in the bush, in that small church late at night, in the chapel of the Franciscan hermitage at Stroud, and fortunately and sustainably for me, in the Eucharist here at St John's Anglican Cathedral in Brisbane among other places, are words written by the Anglican priest and poet, RS Thomas in 'The Absence':

> It is this great absence
> that is like a presence, that compels
> me to address it without hope
> of a reply. It is a room I enter
>
> from which someone has just
> gone, the vestibule for the arrival
> of one who has not yet come.
> I modernise the anachronism
>
> of my language, but he is no more here
> than before. Genes and molecules
> have no more power to call
> him up than the incense of the Hebrews
>
> at their altars. My equations fail
> as my words do. What resource have I
> other than the emptiness without him of my whole
> being, a vacuum he may not abhor?[1]

---

1. 'The Absence', RS Thomas, in *Collected Poems 1945-1990* (London: Phoenix, 2000), 360.

A few years ago, I read that poem at an interfaith dinner and then talked about how for me it captured the nature of what we are trying to honour in our worship at St John's. I then said that I understood that the desire to honour 'the great absence that is like a presence' was something that unified the faiths. Each, I suggested, in their own way, is trying to honour the seemingly oxymoronic presence/absence that RS Thomas refers to in the poem.

At the conclusion of the dinner, Christians from a surprisingly wide variety of denominations, including non-liturgical churches, Muslim, Jewish, and even Buddhist leaders, queued up to ask me for a copy of the poem. Yes, they said, honouring the presence/absence is what we are trying to do. Conversations then ensued about how the various ways of seeking to do that have been shaped by cultural forces, philosophical framing and accidents of history.

The Orthodox Opening to Worship

The Orthodox liturgy begins with some prayers and antiphons that signify the gathering of the people. There is then a ritual element called the Small Entrance, during which the clergy, including the deacon carrying the book of the gospels, enter through the doors of the iconostasis and approach the altar. That is something like the way our Sunday liturgies begin at St John's. The deacon then says words that can be translated, 'Wisdom! Attend!', or 'This is Wisdom. Let us attend!'

'This is Wisdom. Let us attend!' To attend is to be present. It is also to notice what else is present. The Orthodox expect the risen Christ to be present as they celebrate the Divine Liturgy. They expect to encounter Wisdom, Sophia, the feminine, creative principle of the divine. And they intentionally declare that they will attend to the presence of Wisdom and to the presence of Christ. For them worship is a place of expected and anticipated encounter.

Benedictine Practice

When the members of a Benedictine community gather for prayer, they commence by standing still, in silence, for a full minute, a practice they call *statio,* the 'holy pause'. At the end of the prayer service, they do the same thing; they stand in silence for a full minute.

The practise of *statio* is designed to ensure that the community members intentionally stop doing one thing before commencing another. They acknowledge that they have stopped doing the gardening, preparing a meal, studying an interesting topic or having a heated exchange, and become present to prepare for the time of prayer and present to the presence they expect to encounter as they come to prayer. It is about being present in the present, and to the presence that inhabits the present. Then, at the end of the prayer time, they take the time to become present to and for the activity that follows, even if the next activity is the eating of lunch. They seek to be present to the action of eating—to attend to eating, to notice the food, its taste, its texture. How many of us attend to our lunch in that way?

Let us attend. **Statio.**

Concentrating solely on attending is something that we find in Quaker worship, which is nothing like the worship that most of us have in our churches: no set readings, no liturgical texts, no formal homily, no creeds. Just attending and honouring that which is experienced through the attending. As St Francis once said, in a slightly different context, use words only if it is necessary to do so.

Liturgical Churches and Complexity

In more liturgical traditions, our approach to worship is more complex than that practiced by the Quakers. In this paper I want to explore some of the consequences that flow from that complexity and how an awareness of complexity theory might help us negotiate some of the difficult, even wicked, territory we have made for ourselves by having the forms of worship that we do.

In liturgical churches, which interestingly includes churches of the Pentecostal tradition—a claim that many in that tradition find surprising—worship uses a complex of symbols, actions, music and texts to develop and convey meaning, and to create a vessel that at its best holds open a place of encounter, a place where the absence/presence makes itself known. We use the scriptures to tell the story that helps us understand what it is that we are attending to and what is to flow from that. The complex amalgam that is assembled to form worship also provides a space that is used for catechesis, the shaping of fellowship, the forming of the character of the community and the individuals that constitute it and sets the scene for combined action. Western rationalism ensures that worship is also used as an educational space, a doctrinal space and an ideological space. This means that it cannot help but be a political space. It is a truly complex space.

And because it is complex we cannot fully anticipate the effects that worship will have on us or others. Nor can we anticipate the effect of any changes we make to the system that we call worship or liturgy. This provides a particular challenge for those who are into liturgical innovation or renewal, and for those of us who are trying to build safe and inclusive communities.

The Nature of Complex Systems

Dave Snowden, the developer of what is known as the Cynefin Framework,[2] invites us to understand that our world and its systems, organisations and their problems and challenges can be divided into four types. The type of system or problem one is dealing with determines the type of intervention one needs to use to make effective changes to that system.

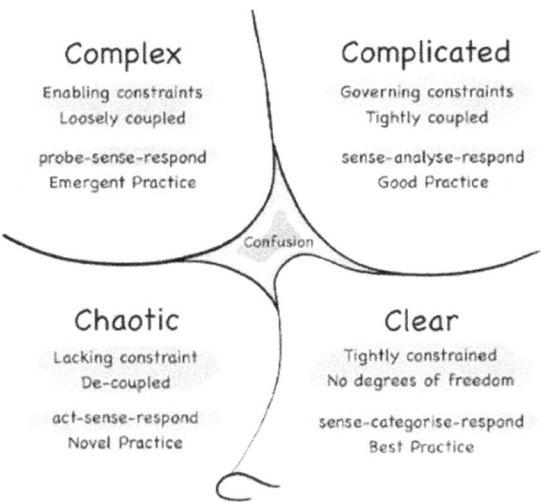

---

2. The Cynefin Company, 'Cynefin Framework', <thecynefin.co/about-us/about-cynefin-framework/?srsltid=AfmBOoqG5DGfM5FoxvooVVw1m70Ud4v94Cw O8PPDt1qB-qM9cMoR7_8a>. Accessed 26 August 2025.

The first type is what the Cynefin Framework names Simple. Simple systems are those in which the processes involved in their operation are clear and describable. These are systems and problems where cause and effect are clearly evident, and so the effect of any intervention is known. And the type of intervention required to achieve an outcome is known. A leaking tap is an example of a simple problem. We know why it is leaking and what needs to be done to fix it. YouTube videos often supply the how as we seek to address simple problems. The notion of 'best practice' applies here.

The second type of system or problem is what is known as Complicated. An airplane is a complicated system. Establishing cause and effect needs expert attention but is discoverable. Complicated systems are the arena in which experts such as engineers operate and in which expertise is required for effective intervention. It is the area governed and documented by operating manuals and the development of 'good practice'.

The third type of system is what is called Complex. These are systems where there are so many moving parts that it is impossible to describe the way the system works. Cause and effect can be observed in hindsight only, and the consequences of tweaking the system can only be described after the fact. Ecosystems, the climate, and most human systems, including the economy are complex.

Those who know they are working in Complex spaces use very different techniques to those operating in Simple and Complicated systems. They exercise what is known as 'emergent practice', that is, they respond to what is emerging from the system, not to what they expect *a priori*, and when intervening in the system they use what are called 'safe to try' or 'safe to fail' small-scale interventions.

The fourth type of system is labelled as Chaotic. The best one can do in a chaotic situation is ride the wave, responding as one can, sometimes just seeking survival. The COVID pandemic created a chaotic system.

In the West we are incredibly good at dealing with Simple and Complicated systems. The technology we all enjoy using is testament to this. The downside is that we are so successful in those two operating arenas we think that we begin to believe the whole world is tameable and manageable, and that every system and problem can be treated as if it is Simple or Complicated. This means that we tend to be very poor at recognising when a system is Complex, or even Chaotic, and so we tend to treat Complex and Chaotic systems as if they are Complicated. So, for example, there have been some inquiries held into the governments' COVID response that have criticised some of what was done. Many of these analyses seem to have assumed that a better way of behaving should have been as evident to those crafting the response as it was to those who were looking at it in hindsight.

There are always lessons to be learnt from such analysis. In fact, as I hope to point out, gathering information is an important thing to be doing, but how we gather it and the presumptions we take into that gathering can affect what we see and learn. Most of this type of analysis treats the problem as if it is Simple or Complicated, and so does not actually teach us much that is useful going forward. We cannot produce best or good practice manuals for dealing with complex or chaotic systems, and any attempt to do so will prevent us from responding to what is actually happening the next time around.

The economy, ecological systems, liturgy and problems like bullying are complex, and our tendency to treat them as if they are merely complicated or even simple means that we continually come up with simple responses that will not work. In recent times we have seen the fruits of this mismatch of system type and response: the ban on children under 16 accessing social media, the 'adult time for adult crime' response to problematic youth here in Queensland, and even our response to climate change. Each of these is a complex problem, also known as a wicked problem, which will require complex societal transformation to address.

Liturgy likewise is a complex system which means that liturgical innovation needs to be approached in a particular way if it is to bear good fruit.

Change and Complexity at Our Best

Tweaking complex systems creates all sorts of unintended consequences, many of which cannot be undone. Since liturgy is a complex system, we can only describe what is emerging. And learn from what we see. So, I will make some observations about what I notice in worship. These will be largely confined to the space I know best: St John's here in Brisbane.

One of the more enduring images I hold of worship at St John's is from one of the times that we were joined by Raymond for a Sunday celebration of the Eucharist. Raymond is a rough sleeper who spends most of his time in West End. We see him on our side of the river once in a while, and occasionally he comes to the Sunday Eucharist with us.

Raymond is a very gentle human being who is very easy to engage in conversation. He also lives with many complex issues and so manages to wash on a very infrequent basis. In the street he is someone people go out of their way to avoid. I understand why they do. They do not know him.

On the Sunday that has come to my mind, Raymond arrived in time for communion and took his place in the communion line and then, kneeling between two regular community members at the altar rail, received communion. I remember their hands, Raymond's with the ground-in dirt of many weeks of living on the streets and the two immaculate pairs of hands on either side, all longing to be fed with the bread of life. I was particularly touched by the way that the regular members did not seek to increase the distance between Raymond and themselves. They were just three people at the Eucharist together.

Over morning tea one of those who had knelt with Raymond at the altar rail engaged him in conversation and introduced him to others. The equality we experienced gathered around the altar was continued over morning tea. The warmth was genuine, even transformative.

At St John's week-by-week at the Eucharist we gather as an incredibly disparate group of people, people who are not brought together by the increasingly narrow sets of criteria that tend to see people gather in our increasingly disconnected world. In that world people know others through their occupation or workplace, or through a narrow, shared interest or an association that requires membership, screening, and the expenditure of money.

Our increasing disconnection from one another means that there are fewer and fewer places where people can be in public and connected, which perhaps has necessitated the development of dating apps. The shopping centre, whilst full of people, is largely a solitary experience. This disconnection has consequences for how we interact and for what it means to be part of society. It is little wonder that there is an increasing amount of 'othering' going on in our political discourse and in the world of social media. People simply do not know other people and so treat them as foreign objects. Few public spaces of interaction remain.

The liturgical life of a place like St John's is one of the few places where a disparate group of people can gather. The space is public. The doors are open. Every Sunday people walk in and out freely while worship is in progress. They can stay if they wish. They leave when they want. We try hard to make everyone welcome.

Our worship and a few of our other activities, such as COWS (Coffee on Wednesdays), which also has a very low entry bar, are among the very few openly available spaces left for encounter with those who are different. These events not only symbolically place us together, but they also give us a unique opportunity to hear the stories of real people and to be transformed by them.

The dynamic I see in operation as people interact in our ever-deepening experience of community reminds me of the transformative process that occurred for participants in the SBS series *Go Back to Where You Came From,* which enabled people who were philosophically opposed to the idea of people seeking asylum to encounter real people seeking asylum. The great majority of participants were softened and transformed by the experience, developing a deeper sense of the complexities, and were moved, to some extent at least, by the humanity of the other. Real people are very different to the images we create in our imaginations. If celebrating liturgy can create this type of outcome, then it is a real blessing. However, the dynamics I have just describe also point us to just how complex is the space in which we are operating.

On the Other Hand

Reading Phyllis Trible *Texts of Terror*[3] while at theological college was a real gift. To have a Baptist scholar punch through the layers of piety that protect the scriptures from scrutiny, and the way they are used from examination, was a real point of liberation for me. As the product description says,

> Professor Trible focuses on four variations upon the theme of terror in the Bible. By combining the discipline of literary criticism with the hermeneutics of feminism, she reinterprets the tragic stories of four women in ancient Israel: Hagar, Tamar, an unnamed concubine, and the daughter of Jephthah.

---

3. Phyllis Trible, *Texts of Terror: Literary-Feminist Readings of Biblical Narratives* (Minneapolis: Fortress Press, 1984).

> In highlighting the silence, absence, and opposition of God, as well as human cruelty, Trible shows how these neglected stories interpreted in memoriam challenge both the misogyny of Scripture and its use in church, synagogue, and academy.

Hagar and her son Ishmael are disposed of, Tamar is raped, the unnamed concubine is given over to the men of Gibeah to be pack raped and beaten, and is then cut into twelve pieces by her master or husband (depending how you read the text), and Jephthah's daughter is killed by her father as a sacrifice to fulfil a vow he made to God in order to win a battle. And it is worth remembering that Jephthah is not just a problem for those who read the Hebrew scriptures, given that the writer of the Letter to the Hebrews describes him as a hero of the faith.[4] Having had Tribble remove the scales from my eyes, I began noticing just how many texts of terror there are and how often we just leave them hanging.

Here are two examples of what this looks like. Firstly, in August of this year, Year B of the lectionary, Ephesians 5:22–24 was read as part of the collection of lections:

> Wives, be subject to your husbands as you are to the Lord. For the husband is the head of the wife just as Christ is the head of the church, the body of which he is the Saviour. Just as the church is subject to Christ, so also wives ought to be, in everything, to their husbands.

We then sang a hymn and heard part of the Bread of Life discourse from the gospel according to John, chapter 6. The preacher chose to focus on John 6, providing a lovely reflection on the Eucharist. The congregation was left to their own devises to process Ephesians 5. Many people find that a troubling text—a troubling text left unaddressed.

The second example came a few years ago, a young man, who is now in formation to be a priest, walked into the cathedral because he had heard about our reputation for being a place dedicated to the pursuit of justice and inclusion with the aim of rekindling his faith. He came specifically to join us for Evening Prayer, and, in part, this is what he heard:

---

4. Heb 11:32

> Then the Lord said to Joshua, 'Stretch out the sword that is in your hand towards Ai; for I will give it into your hand'. And Joshua stretched out the sword that was in his hand towards the city. As soon as he stretched out his hand, the troops in ambush rose quickly out of their place and rushed forward. They entered the city, took it, and at once set the city on fire ... The total of those who fell that day, both men and women, was twelve thousand—all the people of Ai.[5]

The extermination of a city at the Lord's command. An act of self-defence? No, an invader intent on genocide.

'May your word live in us', we said in response to the readings. Welcome to our community. Tell me again about the God you proclaim, Peter.

The Complexity of Liturgy and Worship

Those two stories point to the types of pastoral issues that are created by the complexity of what is on offer when we gather for worship and prayer; offerings we make available to anyone who cares to walk in through our open doors. And having people walk in through our open doors is something we desire.

The complexity that exists in our services of prayer and worship is created in part by the sheer volume of scripture that we encounter in our prayer services and liturgies. It is also created in part by the often-unaddressed complexity of the scriptures themselves. And it is a complexity created by the method we use to choose the readings that will be used in our prayer services and liturgies. A few comments on each of those sources of complexity.

Scripture

The scriptures are a very complex collection of writings. The writings have been shaped by culture; philosophical, theological and anthropological framing; the influence of neighbouring cultures and religions on the communities that created them; the effects of the power plays and influences of empires; the development of agriculture and urbanisation—the list goes on. However, despite

---

5. Josh 8:18–23, 25.

generations of preachers learning about this complexity in seminary and college, a lot of everyday Bible study and preaching approaches the scriptures as if they are simple. The populist idea that all one must do to understand the text is to pick up a copy and read it as if it is a direct and clear communication from God persists.

This largely unacknowledged scriptural complexity adds multiple layers of complexity to what we are doing when we make liturgy. Given that scriptures' complexity is rarely declared in our worship, we are left with gathered communities made up of diverse people with varying perceptions of what scripture is and how it works. This adds another layer of complexity. The hearer hears what the hearer hears. And if the preacher either takes a literalist view or does not address the complexities of the text, negative consequences can flow.

The Volume of Scripture Found in Worship

Given the failure of Marcion's second-century attempt to 'purify' the scriptures, we tend to be deeply suspicious of any system that would see us not attending to the whole of the Bible in worship. And we are deeply suspicious, for very good reasons, of allowing the preacher to choose the text. So, we have very good reasons for why we want to ensure that we attend to the entire collection of the scripture when we come to worship. One of the consequences is that we encounter a huge amount of scripture, gathered from disparate parts of this complex collection, in every liturgy and prayer service. Liturgy provides only a limited amount of time to address the complexities that this introduces to our worship because liturgy is not a Bible study, and treating liturgy as if it is a Bible study and having sermons of forty-five minutes to an hour adds a new level of complexity to worship. Simple solutions to complex problems are always unhelpful.

So, we acknowledge the complexity created by having four pieces of text in a normal Sunday eucharistic liturgy and three, four or five, depending on the number of psalm portions, in the Anglican offices of Morning and Evening Prayer.

The Lectionary

I am a great fan of the *raison d'etre* behind the development of the Revised Common Lectionary (RCL) for the Sunday Eucharist. It was driven by the desire to be honest about the complexity of scripture.

The previous Common Lectionary (CL), which is still in use in many churches, built the first reading found in worship around themes found in the gospel reading for the day. The rhythm of gospel readings is virtually the same across both the RCL and CL. But, in the CL the first readings are chosen to amplify the themes identified by the lectionary compliers in the gospel. As an aside, I note that that method of choosing the other readings involves the application of a simplistic understanding of the gospels to those four complex documents. In the 'Track 1' RCL readings after Pentecost, however, the first readings are not thematically linked to the gospel reading but stand with their integrity intact. This often leads to situations in which the themes of the readings, which are sometimes problematic, vary greatly and have no direct relationship to one another.

An Example of How Complexity Manifests

The introduction of the RCL stands as a testament to how unintended consequences flow when makes changes to a complex system. The RCL was introduced with the very best of intentions in mind. Its introduction has also created a whole new layer of complexity for preacher and congregation alike. I am not advocating for the abandonment of the RCL. Those of us who have been sensitised to its desire to honour the integrity of scripture would be forever distracted by the artificiality of the CL construction should it be reestablished. You cannot go back. You cannot unsee what you have come to see.

Because cause and effect in Complex systems are not linear, one cannot simply undo a change that has been made to the system. The system is altered by the first change. Reversing the change results in further changes to the system. This is why dealing with complex systems requires very different approaches to those used in Simple and Complicated systems. So, we are left with a complex set of diverse and sometimes contradicting texts which the preacher cannot hope to address, which leaves texts of terror and other problematic readings hanging without explanation.

At St John's, people have noticed how the complexity created using RCL can impact people, and we have talked about the consequences of that dynamic in several forums. This has led members of our community to express the desire to have a simple introduction to each of the readings reproduced in the weekly service notes. This has proven to be easier said than done, and we are beginning to doubt if such a resource can exist. Afterall, it would be a simple solution to a complex problem.

Those of us who preach try to be sensitive to that fact that texts of terror do appear as we move through the lectionary. One of our strategies is to ensure that, even if we feel called to address a theme found elsewhere in the lections, that we will address the text of terror in some way. But we are beginning to learn that this simple solution is also not going to address the complexity we face.

Describing More of the Complexity

The problems introduced by scripture do not, of course, capture the complexity encountered in liturgy. The human 'texts' gathered, with their own stories, also introduce dimensions that cannot be addressed with approaches from the Simple and Complicated toolkits.

Trauma

Earlier this year the members of the Cathedral pastoral team spent a morning with a clinical therapist and another person who has been working with them reflecting on the relationship between worship, preaching and trauma. We explored some of the ways that people living with trauma can be triggered by the approach taken by the homilist, the words of hymns, the readings and the words of the liturgy. We canvassed some of the issues that I have already referred to such as the fact that texts of terror can be left hanging.

The session became very interesting when our guests, both of whom had experienced religious trauma, started sharing examples of the approaches they had found helpful for dealing with the texts and homiletic methods that had caused them trauma. It became interesting because many of the proposed solutions proved to be problematic and even triggering for others in the room.

Trauma is complex. Trauma caused by encountering a complex system like worship will always be complex. Being trauma-informed can assist, but in such complex territory we will not always get it right. There are no simple solutions to complex problems.

The Effects of Culture and History

In February of last year, I attended the Tribal Voices Conference run by the now-defunct School of Indigenous Studies in the University of Divinity. As a result, I have had several conversations with First Nations theologians.

Our First Nations theologians are in contact with counterparts in many other parts of the world. They report that Australian churches lag churches in other countries when it comes to advocacy for First Nations people and in the indigenisation of liturgy. They note that the churches and particularly the Anglican Church to which I belong are some of the greatest beneficiaries of the colonisation project.

Australia Day or Invasion Day is possibly the most contentious date in the Australian public calendar. Yet the Anglican Liturgical Committee continues to schedule this a reading for Evening Prayer on that day that includes this passage:

> For the Lord your God is bringing you into a good land, a land with flowing streams, with springs and underground waters welling up in valleys and hills, a land of wheat and barley, of vines and fig trees and pomegranates, a land of olive trees and honey, a land where you may eat bread without scarcity, where you will lack nothing, a land whose stones are iron and from whose hills you may mine copper. You shall eat your fill and bless the Lord your God for the good land that he has given you.[6]

Many of us have advocated with the committee to have this changed. It remains, the committee tells us, because of the call later in the passage not to forget the Lord when enjoying the prosperity of the land. That may well be, but the hearer will hear what the hearer hears. First Nations people hear the colonial overtones.

I mention this simply to demonstrate that societal culture and national history add layers to the complexity of what we are doing in worship. Much of which we simply do not see. But others do.

---

6. Deut 8:7–10.

Evolving Language

Those of us who use liturgical forms use words, lots of words. We cannot avoid using words. The words we use add to the complexity of what we are doing and to what is perceived. When I was preparing an ordination liturgy, I chose a hymn by Australian hymn writer, the Rev'd Dr Elizabeth Smith. The first verse is:

> Praise the God who made our bodies,
> nerve and muscle, flesh and blood,
> made us in God's own true image,
> *male and female,* holy, good.
> Glorify the God who made us!
> Use our bodies to explore
> all the world, with all our senses,
> daily learning more and more.

One of the people I collaborate with in the construction of our liturgies asked if the use of the 'male and female' to define the humanity that holds the image of the divine was consistent with the spirit of the life we are trying to live following the apology to sexuality-diverse and gender-diverse people that was adopted by our synod and delivered in the cathedral last year.

Noting the point, I contacted Elizabeth Smith, who had already addressed the need for revision in the following:

> Praise the God who made our bodies,
> nerve and muscle, flesh and blood,
> made us in God's own true image,
> *holy, wonderful and good.*

The eucharistic liturgy in our 1995 *Prayer Book for Australia* (APBA) also seemed more inclusive when its text adopted the use of 'men and women' in place of the 1978 version's 'made man in your own image' and 'you bound yourself to mankind'.[7] These days the members of my team are updating the words as we preside with phrases such as 'all people' and 'you made us, in our glorious diversity, in your own image'. So not only does language adds layers of complexity, but the evolution of language does too.

---

7. *A Prayer Book for Australia* (Mulgrave, VIC: Broughton Books, 1995), 159.

And into that complex mix we need to add the fact that we, for good reason, develop deep attachments to texts and so tend to preserve them. So, 'Lead us not into temptation' survives in the text of the Lord's Prayer used in many churches some thirty-five years after the English Language Liturgical Consultation adopted 'Save us from the time of trial' in 1988.

Where to from Here?

I hope I have been able to establish that our liturgical life needs to be understood and therefore interacted with as a complex system. A simple solution to the problems that arise from the complex nature of worship would be to adopt Quaker practice. But given that this would be simple answer to a complex problem it would not achieve the result for which one might hope.

Those of us who are fed and nourished by complex forms of worship, systems of symbol, music and colour would find that we did not have a rewarding experience. For me, whilst contemplation and silence are very valuable parts of my spiritual practice, the Eucharist is where it is at for me. Simplistic solutions to complex problems never work.

So, what I am advocating is developing an understanding of complexity theory and how to operate in complex systems which might assist us to, firstly, deal with some of the consequences of the complex system in which we operate and, secondly, shape how we intervene in the system when we do liturgical reform and development.

Attending: Learning What Is Going On

Our interactions with those who presented the trauma workshop remind us that we need to be attending all the time to what is happening in worship and how it is affecting people. Whilst we cannot hope to gather all the information available, reflection and faith formation groups allow us to monitor some of what is happening for people and what the real effect of worship on them might be. This will shift over time even if the liturgy does not change, as the evolution in the meaning, weight and effect of words will see things change continually. The process of gathering this information is called sensing, and the process of reflecting on that information is called sense-making.

For those of us who enact and create liturgy, the process of attending may require some shift in emphasis in terms of our processes. Take the example of the Australia Day lections. Whether the current lections should be used and are effective does not depend on what the Liturgical Committee thinks it should mean to the reader but rather on what the reader/hearer makes of them.

A sense-making process would see the committee taking on board that First Nation peoples, their allies, and even people who wish to celebrate the colonial project all hear the Joshua text as affirming colonisation. If this is not their intention, then they would reflect on what they have learnt, seek to find an alternate text that speaks to the theme of not forgetting God in the face of abundance, introduce that text as an experimental measure, seek feedback about how it was working for people through some more intentional sense-making, and then either adopt the alternate text as 'permanent'—that is, until it no longer works effectively—or try another alternate text.

Intervening in Complex Systems[8]

What I have just described, sense-making, experiment, further sense-making, repeat, is a classic example of how one intervenes in a complex system. Complex systems by their nature require us to attend closely and to notice that which is emerging. We cannot know up front what effect any change to the system will have because we do not fully know how the system works. There are forces and processes at play that we do not know about and so when we make interventions the system can respond in ways that surprise us.

---

8. Image by Edward Stoop, <https://commons.wikimedia.org/w/index.php?curid=53810658>. Accessed 26 August 2025.

Because we do not know how the system will respond, it is important that we do not make major interventions in the system, but rather do what are called 'safe to fail' or 'safe to try' experiments. Hallmarks of these experiments will be that they involve grassroots or end-user participation, use intentional methods for gaining feedback, and take heed of the context and of what the guardrails should be. These are known in the complexity nomenclature as the Enabling Constraints.

Enabling Constraints are rules that limit actions in complex systems to encourage innovation and novelty. They are often used in situations where rules are unclear, goals are difficult to define, and there is a lot of uncertainty. In our Anglican context the enabling constraints include that any liturgical form must be consistent with the Book of Common Prayer, which is constitutionally our standard of worship. Other enabling constraints might be the biblical narratives of the institution of the Eucharist, the historical forms of the Eucharist, the prayer of Hippolytus, and the Didache.

In our Anglican Church we saw something of a sense-making process, albeit truncated, at work during our process of liturgical reform in the late 1980s and early 1990s. As we moved towards the adoption of the 1995 APBA, the Liturgical Committee issued several experimental rites and texts for the offices and asked the church to use them and send feedback. The feedback was used to recast the rites into the text that was taken to the 1995 General Synod for adoption. I say that the process was truncated because the revised rites were not road tested before being taken to Synod, so many of us were surprised and disappointed when the APBA came out.

Attending to Context on the Way Forward

Another of the enabling constraints that allows for effective intervention in Complex Systems is the context in which the system operates, exploring the context and getting to know the context. One model that I think could be helpful for forming an understanding of context is one that could be based on what Sarah Coakley calls the development of a *théologie totale*, the nature of which she begins to explore in the first work in her theological summa, *God, Sexuality, and the Self: An Essay 'On the Trinity'*.[9]

---

9. Sarah Coakley, *God, Sexuality, and the Self: An Essay 'On the Trinity'* (Cambridge, UK: Cambridge University Press, 2013).

Sarah Coakley advocates for the development of a *théologie totale* as a response to what Kirsten Guidero describes as 'a number of current theological confusions, struggles, or dead ends'. Guidero continues,

> While these crises take various shapes, they generally cluster around perceived clashes between Christian 'orthodoxy' and challenges stemming from post-Enlightenment 'secular' approaches to social sciences, philosophy, political thought, gender, and sexuality. Coakley observes that responses to these debates often take shape as mutually exclusive options that tend to cast themselves as authentic spirituality without adequately exploring the historical resources offered by Christian spirituality.[10]

Sarah Coakley suggests that developing a *théologie totale* would begin to address this impasse. A *théologie totale* would seek to incorporate the best understanding of who we are and what the earth and its systems are from biology, sociology, psychology and so on. In other words, it would allow us to begin to understand our context, what it is to be human and embodied, what it means to live where we live and to understand something of the community in which we find ourselves, and to which we ultimately want to have something helpful to say. Above all, she suggests this understanding of context will be shaped and deepened through our life of prayer and worship. So, it would involve a sort of feedback loop where worship informs context, and context informs the way worship develops.

---

10. Kirsten Guidero, 'Review of Sarah Coakley, *God, Sexuality, and the Self: An Essay "On the Trinity"*, *Journal of Scriptural Reasoning* 17:1 (August 2018), <jsr.shanti.virginia.edu/back-issues/vol-17-no-1-august-2018-special-issue-on-re-enchantment-and-scriptural-reasoning/review-of-sarah-coakley-god-sexuality-and-the-self-an-essay-on-the-trinity>. Accessed 26 August 2025.

'The Congregation Is Not an Audience': Expanding the Meaning of Participation in Worship

Matthew Julius

Matthew Julius is a graduate of Pilgrim Theological College in Melbourne and is the Assembly Advocate for Transforming Worship in the Uniting Church in Australia. He works as Church Engagement Worker for Uniting, the community services organisation of the Uniting Church in Victoria and Tasmania.

Abstract

The theme of participation in worship has deep roots in the Christian tradition, giving shape to the word used to refer to Christian worship: 'liturgy'. Drawing on its etymological roots, 'liturgy' might be rendered as 'work of the people,' or perhaps 'public works'—leaning more on the connection to the Greek for 'public' (*leitos*) rather than 'people' (*laos*). The public dimension of the church's work recalls the way Jesus' own ministry was marked by public engagement with various crowds. The public work—that is, liturgy—of the church consists in making public an encounter with Christ. This claim implies that the congregation is not an audience but is invited into full participation in the church's work. The account of participation offered by this paper cuts across considerations of the congregation's activity or passivity: the fullness of Christ's encounter with the world demands all manner of participation within and outside the liturgical gathering itself. Drawing on social theory, art, and music theory this paper proposes an account of participation which expands outwards beyond the liturgical gathering to the social context of the assembly and turns inwards to the subjective transformation of those who worship.

'. . . but for those outside, everything comes in parables; in order that "they may indeed *be an audience*, but not understand" . . . ' (Mk 4:11–12)

'If a tree falls in a forest, and no one is there to hear it, does it make a sound?'
—attributed to Bishop George Berkeley

Introduction

The theme of participation in worship has deep roots in the Christian tradition, giving shape to the word used to refer to Christian worship itself: 'liturgy'. Drawing on its etymological roots, 'liturgy' might be rendered as 'work of the people', or perhaps 'public works'—leaning more on the connection to the Greek for 'public' (*leitos*) rather than 'people' (*laos*). The public dimension of the church's work recalls the way Jesus' own ministry was marked by public engagement with various crowds. These crowds came to hear him preach, feel his healing touch, taste his generous feasts, see his power over demons, and these include the wise women and men who brought perfume for his body. In this regard, the public works of Jesus can serve as a helpful guide for considering the church's ongoing public works, within a rich and expansive understanding of Christ's body. The central claim driving this essay is that the public work—that is, liturgy—of the church consists in making public an encounter with Christ. This claim implies that the congregation is not an audience but is invited into full participation in the church's work. Such participation precedes and cuts across considerations of the congregation's activity or passivity: the fullness of Christ's encounter with the world demands both active and passive participation, within and outside the liturgical gathering itself. Participation in the church's public work does, however, require the recognition of the connection between the presence of Christ in liturgy, and the ineluctable relationality of Christ's body. The congregation is not an audience, they are instead the public works department, serving under the governing body of Christ.

The suggestion that the congregation is often an audience (and implicitly here: ought not be) commonly refers to an image offered by the Danish poet, thinker and theologian Søren Kierkegaard. Kierkegaard offers an analogy for worship as a play consisting of actors, prompts, and an audience, in order to contrast two accounts of Christian worship.[1] The first account, which Kierkegaard thinks is the primary one operating in the church of his day (and we might say of our own day too) sees the priest and lay leaders as the actors, God through the Holy Spirit is the prompter, and the congregation are the audience. Against this Kierkegaard offers an account which sees the congregation themselves as the actors, the priest and lay leaders as the prompters, and God as the audience of this play. While this image has been subject to criticism and adaptation,[2] it nevertheless identifies the contours of a common reality. In this reality the congregation functions as if they were a passive audience attending a performance, and points towards an alternative wherein the congregation take on a more active role. This paper seeks to nuance this image in three important ways, by sitting alongside this initial image from Kierkegaard and three others.

The first image also comes again from Søren Kierkegaard—though much less cited in liturgical studies—and highlights the ambiguity of the value of action within and beyond the liturgy. Drawing on the parabolic nature of Jesus' teachings, this section highlights that the 'who' of the church's public work belies unstable boundaries. The 'public' of the assembly cannot straightforwardly be marked by visible active participation but is constituted by inward subject transformation through an encounter with Christ. We must insist on an ambiguity about who constitutes 'the public' of the church's public work and think more seriously about the other *publics* (plural) and indeed counter-publics who are implicitly addressed by the church's public work.

The second image, from the Dutch quotidian painter Johannes Vermeer, helps to move beyond the simple binary of passivity and activity as roles for the public assembly. Can we move beyond conceiving of the Christian assembly as either a passive 'audience' or active 'players', without being reduced to pietism and while maintaining a grounding in Christ's initiating action in the liturgy? This section explores an answer to this question by reflecting on three senses of Christ's presence among the assembly.

---

1. Referenced in Stephen Burns, *Liturgy* (SCM Studyguide), second edition (London: SCM Press, 2018), 8.
2. See for example Kevin Van Hoozer, *The Drama of Doctrine: A Canonical-Linguistic Approach to Christian Theology* (Louisville, KY: Westminster John Knox, 2005).

The final image—a slight stretch on the theme—is conceptual: Adapting an idea from music theory, this final section highlights the broader social relationality which enables the liturgical event. This is an image in which each plays their respective part but invites a more expansive understanding of the kinds of parts each might play—beyond the narrow time and space of the liturgy itself. What needs to be considered, in other words, may not be *whether* the congregation functions as an audience but how each member of the assembly finds their place and in what manner. This 'finding one's place' pushes beyond questioning the status of the congregation as audience or actors: It is not simply that the congregation might shift from being a watcher and listener to a player in the work, but the work itself must move beyond watching and listening, to embrace the full presence of Christ and Christ's body in and for the world. It is this embrace which truly makes public the central work of Christ: 'that coming reconciliation and renewal which is the end in view for the whole creation'.[3]

'Getting' the Joke: The Unstable Boundaries of Jesus' Giggle Kingdom

The first image to set alongside the framing image from the introduction also comes from Søren Kierkegaard, in his interpretation of the biblical story of Abraham's sacrifice of Isaac: *Fear and Trembling*. Kierkegaard offers an image of a preacher whose parishioner, taking a sermon on the Abraham story with utmost seriousness, goes home to murder his own son.[4] The preacher, summoning his authority and indignation, rebukes this parishioner for such an obviously evil act. Kierkegaard points out that there is a sort of tragic comedy to this whole affair: After all, the parishioner was merely putting into practice the lesson from the sermon not to withhold one's best from God. (Truly the 'liturgy beyond the liturgy'.) Kierkegaard goes on to note how much more tragic and comedic it would be if the preacher had not responded with a rebuke to the parishioner, but with self-congratulation for preaching what was clearly an excellent and effective sermon! (If only parishioners put into action our other

---

3. 'Basis of Union', Uniting Church in Australia, para. 3, <https://uniting.church/basisofunion>. Accessed 14 April 2025.
4. Søren Kierkegaard, *Fear and Trembling*, translated by Alastair Hannay (London: Penguin Books, 2003), 58–59.

sermons so readily.) Activity spurred on by liturgical participation, however, may not always have beneficial effects. The point which this story serves for Kierkegaard—writing under the pseudonym Johannes de Silentio (John the Silent)—is that the parishioner failed to understand that religious truth always carries with it an important element of irony.[5] The layered meanings of ironic communication are a key part of how religious truth affects not only outward actions but invokes inward (subjective) transformation.

Of course, pastors and preparers of liturgy hope that liturgical participation may also have beneficial effects. Sermons do not only lead to bloodletting. But before moving too quickly to accounts of action spurred on by liturgy, or developing normative frameworks which might constrain the liturgy beyond the liturgy, a prior question presents itself: Who are we as participants in liturgical action? And perhaps more importantly: Who do we become? In Kierkegaard's long-standing fascination with irony (the subject of his master's thesis[6]), his concern is with the relationship between irony and subjective transformation. It is this second question about who we become—more so than a direct concern with ethics or even with existential praxis—which concerns Kierkegaard, and ought to concern liturgical inquiry about participation.

In the witnesses we receive in scripture, Jesus' teaching has often been understood to contain its own share of irony through the use of parables, which behove themselves to a variety of treatments.[7] The possible layers of meaning recorded in the text, and the fact that these texts themselves rework a more originary memory for later audiences, mean that Jesus' teaching cannot be construed simply as a ministry to 'the public' he addressed. The original source texts behind the received text spoke to a particular audience (the identity of which is lost in any fine detail); the collated texts served an original audience, and the reception history (not to mention the status of the text as scripture) implies yet more audiences throughout history and place.

---

5. *The Concept of Irony* was the subject of Keirkegaard's final dissertation at the University of Copenhagen.
6. Søren Kierkegaard, *The Concept of Irony*, translated by Howard V. Hong and Edna H. Hong (Princeton, NJ: Princeton University Press, 1989).
7. Joachim Jeremias, *The Parables of Jesus,* translated by SH Hooke (London: SCM Press, 1958), 17–18.

The parabolic nature of Jesus' recorded teachings, and the rise and fall in the various crowds' disposition towards Jesus, suggest not simply various audiences but perhaps a series of different 'publics'. The public dynamics in Jesus' ministry can be seen in the traces they leave in Mark's gospel, distinctly marked by the theme of the 'messianic secret': the motif that certain figures throughout the text apprehend Jesus' identity, though it is withheld from public proclamation until the crucifixion.[8] Mark offers a rather cryptic framing of Jesus' ministry with the parable of the sower, which functions as a teaching about Jesus' own teaching. In this parable, from the fourth chapter of Mark, a sower sows seed on various types of soil, resulting in various levels of success in cultivating a crop. It is the interpretation of this parable, however, which is key. Jesus is recorded as saying,

> To you has been given the secret of the kingdom of God, but for those outside, everything comes in parables; in order that 'they may indeed look, but not perceive, and may indeed listen, but not understand; so that they may not turn again and be forgiven' (Mark 4:11–12, emphasis added).

Far from the clear and effective preacher of Kierkegaard's *Fear and Trembling*, the Jesus of Mark's gospel teaches in such a way that there is an intentional split within the crowd themselves. A distinction is made between those who 'get' the proclamation which Jesus sows—much like 'getting' a joke—and subsequently experience subjective transformation, and those who do not. The gospels embody this distinction through the construction of representative publics throughout the narratives, such as the various groups of religious leaders—scribes, Pharisees—and exemplary disciple figures.

Writing in quite a different context, social theorist Michael Warner identifies a multiplicitous sense of 'public' in the amorphous spaces which challenges naive notions about the totality of all people ('the general public'). Warner pays particular attention to minoritised 'publics', particularly in the context of public health

---

8. This motif within Mark was first studied in depth by William Wrede in *The Messianic Secret* (Cambridge, UK: James Clarke & Co, 2021). Examples of similar dynamics could otherwise be drawn from Jesus' long pseudo-private asides in John's gospel, the distinctly apocalyptic parables of Matthew's gospel, or the disruptive acts of table fellowship in Luke.

message amidst the HIV/AIDS crisis of the 1980s and early 1990s.[9] Publics arise out of a relationship to 'texts [broadly construed] and their circulation'.[10] Publics are the constructed audience of a text, which is neither reducible to the immediate audience of a text in any given performance, viewing, or reading, nor extensively inclusive of all possible people whatsoever who might encounter the text in question. Rather, to talk about the public of a text is to consider who the text imagines it is speaking to in its deployment of language, images, concepts, and so on. Further, it is to consider how the text's transmission opens the possibility of some people engaging with it, and others not: Who is being targeted by the distribution of the text? As a text's history unfolds it will be engaged by many who do not fit the typological public implied by the text itself. It is this which in turn gives rise to what Warner calls 'counter-publics'.[11]

This dynamic of publics and counter-publics can be seen as at play within the biblical texts themselves—when the teachings of Jesus are treated as texts in their own right within the narrative world of the gospel texts—and in the reception history of biblical texts, of which contemporary Christians and others are a part. In this way we can see that just as the various publics stood in various relationships with Jesus throughout the gospel narratives, so too are various publics and counter-publics generated by the church's own contemporary public works. Thus, liturgy is not simply the work of the constituted people of the church, the work of the church as a public, but in its very enactment *presumes* a public as its participants and audience.

Liturgical scholars are attuned to this in discussions of culture and context through their attention to the use of particular language, texts, practices, and the social realities of the congregation in which liturgical assemblies are gathered: the use of a formal register of language; English as *lingua franca*; the requirement to use a particular hymnbook; scripted prayers from particular source books; how, where and whether invitation to the liturgical gathering is offered. All of these do not simply exhibit what kind of public is at work in the doing of the liturgy; as a text itself, these liturgical realities imply a certain construction of a public *for* whom this public work addressed.

---

9. Michael Warner, 'Publics and Counterpublics', *Public Culture* 14/1 (2002): 49–50.
10. Warner, 'Publics and Counterpublics', 50.
11. Warner, 'Publics and Counterpublics', 81.

This recognition of the multiple sense of the meaning of 'public' within the context of the church's public work qualifies the idealised image of liturgical participation offered at the start of this essay. While the *Westminster Catechism* might suggest that our chief human end is to 'worship God and enjoy [God] forever', this does not mean that in the meantime our fellow human beings are not also in attendance at our liturgical performances. The point here is to note that alongside discussions of how our liturgical activity is shaped by and in turn shapes our understanding of God, and who we are as a people, the church's public work also constructs a negative space of a particular public as an intended audience—and thus as invited participants into the encounter with Christ.

Jesus' own ministry disrupted who within the public 'got' what he had to say, and so experienced subjective transformation. This witness from Jesus' ministry challenges us to be attentive to what kinds of counter-publics might be necessary to disrupt the *gestalt* (irreducible view of the whole) implied by our public work.

Mary, Martha and the Messiah Walk into a House . . .

The second image offered alongside the image of the overly literal parishioner from *Fear and Trembling* is the following image by the Dutch painter Johannes Vermeer, famous for his depictions of everyday settings.

Johannes Vermeer *Christ in the House of Martha and Mary*, Oil on Canvas, c.1655, Scottish National Gallery, Edinburgh

Mary and Martha are two examples of figures in the gospels who concretise the dynamics identified in the previous section. Vermeer's depiction of this story captures Jesus resting in the house of Mary and Martha. The passive Mary sits and listens to Jesus, while her sister Martha is actively cleaning and preparing the table (Luke 10:38–42). One of the key features in Vermeer's image is the juxtaposition of Martha, leaning over the table holding a loaf of bread, and Mary, who is engrossed in the teaching of the bread of life. Analysing the image, the restful posture of Mary is mirrored in Jesus himself, whose body reclines in the chair. Here Jesus is portrayed at rest in the mundane domestic setting of Vermeer's day. This image suggests that to 'get' the teaching of Jesus (in the sense above) might mean to allow Christ's presence to rest in the assembly. The standard interpretation of this passage emphasises precisely this point, that Mary is the one who 'gets' it, while Martha does not. We are right to be suspicious of this interpretation alongside feminist critiques which note the denigration of 'women's work' in this scene.

This critique of the standard interpretation might give us fresh eyes to see that in Vermeer's painting Jesus' role is not simply to validate the posture of Mary but to function as the hinge point within the image connecting Mary and Martha: the active and the passive, the one who hears the word and the one who brings the bread. This unity is only possible because it begins by entering the encounter with the resting presence of Christ, as the eye follows the line of Mary's sight towards Jesus' face and then towards Martha.

There is also a counter-line through which the viewer's eye might move: following the movement back from Martha, through the bread, towards Jesus and following Jesus' hand extended towards Mary. Juxtaposed with the bread, and the literal figure of Jesus, we might note a three-fold representation of the body of Christ, as if Jesus is pointing towards Mary saying, 'this is my body'. The point here is to note a possible connection between the resting presence which enables Christ to be fully present, and the resting presence of Christ which enables Mary (here the paradigmatic disciple) to be fully present (and setting aside questions of relating the presence of Christ and the bread).

Do our liturgical practices reflect this three-fold vision of the presence of Christ in the assembly? Not only an attempt to invoke the presence of Christ in mystical, spiritual, or eucharistic terms, but also the full presence of Christ's body in the assembly? Such presence of Christ's body may mean precisely the disruption of who we think we are, or who we implicitly think should be there by virtue of the forms and norms of our liturgical practice.

We might ask, when we think of epiclesis as an invocation of the Spirit's presence, which and whose human needs are articulated as the necessary human corollary into which the Spirit is called? The Spirit is, of course, never absent and in need of conjuring (we probably have little power to command the direction of the blowing wind in any case), but the epicletic call is an expression of human need and desire. How are our epicletic calls shaped by the form of our human need and desire? And whose human need and desire? We might consider how an epiclesis within the Great Prayer of Thanksgiving might be set into a different contextual cosmology, for example, addressing a different implied public even as this called is addressed to God:

> Send us your Spirit
> from deep within the land
> that this grain from the soil,
> and this fruit from the vine
> might sign and seal our creaturely communion with you
> in the family of all things *(author's composition)*.

Or perhaps in epiclesis the yearnings of our hearts might draw from our everyday lives, for which the resting presence of Christ is the salve. In as much as we seek after the resting presence of Christ, we ought also to seek after the full presence of Christ's body, particularly for those who are excluded by the curtailed welcome implicit in our liturgical acts—those precisely to whom Christ paradigmatically points and says, 'this is my body'. Such full presence of the body may not be marked necessarily by particular forms of activity but may in both activity and passivity reflect again that subjective transformation of 'getting' the presence of Christ. The figure of Jesus in Vermeer's painting reflects this ambivalence towards activity and passivity, holding together the respective work of the two sisters. To raise the everyday to a theological point: the presence of Christ transfigures both sitting to listen and fussing at the table into hearing the Word and celebrating a sacramental meal.

Vermeer's placing this image in the concrete domestic setting of his day makes the point: the question of 'getting' the encounter with Christ is how Jesus meets us here, in the everyday, in our concrete lived experience. It is the connections we make between the everyday lives of those excluded by the liturgy, who approach the liturgy as counterpublics, which truly invites the presence of Christ to rest in our midst. My own tradition's desire to set scripture within the broader life of the church might point us to this end, in the Uniting Church's

Basis of Union: 'The Word of God on whom salvation depends is to be heard and known from Scripture appropriated in the worshipping and witnessing life of the Church'.[12]

The teaching of Jesus points to deeper dynamics present in the entirety of Jesus' public works, not simply in intimate moments of teaching but appropriated across Christ's own public worshipping and witnessing life. In this life the assumptions regarding insiders and outsiders in God's new work are disrupted and so imply ambiguous boundaries for the new people formed by the kingdom of God which the Messiah proclaims. Taken as a model for the church's contemporary public work, the task is to attend to how the church's work invites people to 'get' the joke of Christian proclamation. Anchoring the question of participation in this layered meaning of Jesus' teaching and public ministry helpfully cuts across an assumption that participation can easily be equated with activity in the liturgy (or a result of it). While participation *may* mean a more active role for the congregation in liturgical gatherings, such activity should be aimed towards the seeking after the resting presence of Christ, and so the full presence of Christ's body within the assembly. This requires a more expansive understanding of participation, and the broader *contexts* (always plural and always interacting dynamically with each other) in which people live their everyday lives. It is the integral relationship between the liturgy and the social realities always embedded within it, and within which it is always embedded, which help us properly understand participation. To think this through more clearly, we turn to our last conceptual image, taken from music theory.

Liturgicking: Smuggling Participants into Public Works

In the field of music theory, Christopher Small developed the idea of 'musicking'.[13] Small advocates that we expand our understanding of music beyond dots on a page or even vibrations in the air and begin to include the full range of factors which shape what music is and how it is performed, not simply how we make music but how we *do* music, our musicking of the performative event. For Small, to talk thoroughly about music means considering the full range of ways in which people take part in a performance:

---

12. 'Basis of Union', para. 5.
13. Christopher Small, *Musicking: The Meanings of Performing and Listening* (Hanover, CT: University Press of New England, 1998).

> We might at times even extend [musicking's] meaning to what the person is doing who takes the tickets at the door or the heft men who shift the piano and the drums or the roadies who set up the instruments and carry out the sound checks or the cleaners who clean up after everyone else has gone. They, too, are all contributing to the nature of the event that is a musical performance. . . . The act of musicking establishes in the place where it is happening a set of relationships, and it is in those relationships that the meaning of the act lies.[14]

These considerations might further consider the setting in which the music is performed; the norms around the audience's behaviour (does the audience dance, or sing along, or sit quietly?); the behaviour of the performers (stilted, dancing, formal, casual, improvisational?); the accessibility of the performance (are tickets sold, for how much? what social strata are included? is there physical access for people with impaired mobility or who use mobility aids?); and the media through which the music is received, including digital and livestreamed. All these aspects—and more—are included in Small's category of 'musicking'. This is an attempt to acknowledge that music as an event is a gathering place of a broader social reality, a set of actions and relationships which extend across place and time, notably with ambiguous boundaries.

Transposed into the discussion of Christian liturgy—and a possible notion of 'liturgicking'—the insight of musicking leads us beyond the words, gestures, rituals, and so on, which constitute a liturgical gathering (and which often exercise discussions within liturgical studies). Instead, we are led to reflect on how every aspect of the liturgical gathering, even a seemingly passive congregation, serves to shape the reality of the liturgical event. This seems at first glance an uninteresting point: A liturgical event is what it is by virtue of what it is.

The point, however, is that the emphasis Small makes on the ineluctable relationality of musicking suggests that the relational core of the liturgical event is also of central importance. Set in this conceptual frame, the final image encompasses the relational whole

---

14. Small, *Musicking*, 8, 13, cited in Swee Hong Lim, 'Methodologies of Musicking in Practical Theology: Portal into the World of Contemporary Worship Song', *International Journal of Practical Theology*, 18/2 (2014): 305–16 at 307.

which is the totality of the congregation's social relatedness—within itself and beyond—in their liturgicking. This implies, recalling the unstable boundaries of the assembly's constitutive publics and counterpublics, also an ambiguous extension through time. That is, the boundaries of the assembly constituted by any given liturgical event are not only ambiguous in terms of who 'gets' what's going on but also ambiguous in terms of *when* they participate. The ever-passive Bob, who never seems to pay attention to the sermon but nonetheless dutifully maintains the guttering along the brick facade, may perhaps not enact his part of the liturgical happening until later in the week—when he gets round to it. Each of these vital tasks: Maintenance and just sitting there shape the reality of the liturgical event.

Considering what it means to promote participation within the liturgy should go beyond the limited vocabulary found in liturgical scripts and rubrics (and for the sake of my own tradition, even the 'blubrics' printed in blue ink in UCA resources). It must be mindful that the public work of liturgy implicitly creates both a public, to whom the liturgy as text might be understood to be addressed, and various counter-publics, whose full presence may be circumscribed in various ways. Limiting the markers of participation to activity within the liturgical hour may not be sufficient. Rather, discussions of participation in liturgy ought to consider how the Word of God is appropriated in our broader worshipping and witnessing lives, how our public work acts in concert with our work in the public realm of everyday life, which surely is the true domain of anything worth being called 'public theology'.

This broader notion of participation leads to the ineluctable relationality of liturgy: relationships whose shape have far more to do with everyday life than roles served at church. Such an exploration of the church's liturgicking relativises the concrete practices of liturgy and ought to make these truly responsive to the broader relationality of the church's common life as a part of the world. For the full presence of Christ's body to be present in liturgy, assemblies must recognise the full presence of Christ on both the holy tables we gather around in worship *and* the common tables of our everyday lives which are made holy by the Christ who comes to rest at them with us. It is this movement between the realities of everyday life and the wider communal life of the church, and the public work of the church as assembly where true participation is found.

Stopping

It is not enough to interrogate whether the congregation is a passive audience when the assembly is gathered. We must acknowledge that whether passive or active, whether people 'get' it on a Sunday morning (or at whatever time the people meet), each must take their part in the community that finds its centre in the liturgical event. This liturgical event is not marked by weekly ritual but by the double movement of Christ's resting presence and the full presence of Christ's body. In this sense participation is no longer an aspiration but a proclamation, because indeed Jesus' public work is for the sake of the world, that all may be reconciled and renewed. What we need to 'get', after all, is not simply that we might all have a turn or fulfil a presider's anguishing desire not to die in awkward silence. What we need to 'get' is that we ourselves are gotten, received, grasped by Christ in all the myriad ways we share in the far kingdom of Christ's reign. This is the life of the congregation, and it is this interstitial community which enacts the public works of God—where Christ is pleased to dwell.

Eucharistic Concelebration Within a Synodal Church: What Is Appropriate Today?

Paul Taylor

Paul Taylor is Assistant Director of the ACU Centre for Liturgy and Organist and Director of Music at Sacred Heart Cathedral, Bendigo, Victoria.

Abstract

The practice of large-scale concelebration at Mass is one that often leads to discussion in liturgical contexts because of the impact this ritual practice can have on perceptions of the liturgy (particularly by women) and the distorted emphasis it can place upon particular ministers, such as the clergy. This article explores the historical precedents for concelebration in church tradition, the liturgical norms for its use in the post-conciliar era (including some apparent reservations of Pope St Paul VI as recounted by Archbishop Annibale Bugnini), and also some suggestions today for limiting the numbers of concelebrants in large-scale eucharistic celebrations, particularly within a Synodal Church context, which seeks to achieve a more effective ministerial collaboration between clergy, religious and laity.

Introduction

The practice of eucharistic concelebration has become a relatively common custom within the Roman Catholic tradition. The practice involves one or more ordained priests vested in an alb with a coloured stole, and sometimes with a chasuble, standing near the main celebrant of the Mass during the eucharistic prayer and sharing in some ritual actions. These include reciting the words of institution of Christ at the Last Supper and extending hands during the epiclesis, or calling down the Holy Spirit over the gifts of bread and wine. This current practice can be traced to the Second Vatican Council (1962–1965), which restored eucharistic concelebration within the Catholic Church.

The current practice of concelebration is sometimes a source of tension between those in favour (bishops and priests) and those against it or who have reservations (a cohort of clergy, religious and laity). Whilst there are different perspectives regarding concelebration, the focus of this article is *large-scale* concelebrations involving dozens to hundreds of concelebrants within the context of a Synodal Church. What is appropriate today? A suitable context for this question is outlined below.

Historical Background

Eucharistic concelebration has a long history, with roots in scripture and the early Christian communities. Whilst relatively rare in the first part of the twentieth century, the reintroduction of eucharistic concelebration at the Second Vatican Council has been documented by Italian Archbishop Annibale Bugnini (1912–1982), one of the principal architects of the council's liturgical changes, who served as the secretary of the Consilium for the implementation of the conciliar reforms and who worked closely with Pope Paul VI (1897–1978).[1]

Before examining Bugnini's perspective, it is useful to look back for a guide to the early precursors of concelebration in the Eastern and the Western liturgical traditions. It is also important to define some terms and recall what liturgical historian Robert Taft has noted: technically, concelebration can refer to *any liturgical celebration* whereby the local community of the baptised celebrates its common profession and mystery of the Christian faith. Taft goes on to say that, originally, concelebration was a practice whereby priests participated in the liturgy of their bishop.[2] However, within the Eastern and Western liturgical traditions, Taft has identified three main types of concelebration:

---

1. See Annibale Bugnini, 'Concelebration' in *The Reform of the Liturgy: 1948–1975* (Collegeville, MN: The Liturgical Press, 1990), 123*ff*.
2. Robert F Taft, 'Concelebration' in *The HarperCollins Encyclopedia of Catholicism*, edited by Richard McBrien (New York: HarperCollins, 1995), 341.

1. Sacramental verbal co-consecration in the current Roman Rite, whereby certain words (the institution narrative) are prayed simultaneously by the main celebrant and concelebrants nearby, a practice shared by the Byzantine, Coptic, Maronite, and increasingly the Armenian and Syro-Malabar traditions;
2. Distributive concelebration, used in Armenian, Coptic, East and West Syrian and Ethiopian traditions, where more than one minister shares in the liturgical prayers and actions, including parts of the eucharistic prayer, but not at the same time as the main celebrant (especially the consecration);
3. Coordinated concelebration, whereby each priest consecrates his own bread and wine at a separate altar. This is permitted within the West Syrian and Ethiopian rites, and is more an example of synchronised, multiple celebrations of the Eucharist, rather than concelebration in the technical sense.

The focus of this article will be on the first type: sacramental verbal co-consecration.

Scriptural Roots and Liturgical Traditions

Some liturgical scholars suggest that in the New Testament there are possible references to concelebration in the First Timothy (4:14), where St Paul refers to the gift Timothy received through the laying on of hands not just from one presbyter but from the whole council of elders.[3] Sometime later, according to the testimonies of early church communities, there are a number of references that liturgical scholars have cited as precursors of contemporary eucharistic concelebration.[4]

In the first century, Clement of Rome refers to a celebration of the Eucharist with various ministries present (namely, bishop, presbyters, deacons and laity). A century later, Ignatius of Antioch refers to the unity of the eucharistic celebration by one bishop at the one altar surrounded by presbyters and deacons. The third-century *Apostolic Tradition*, attributed to Hippolytus in Rome, refers to deacons

---

3. Paul Turner, *Ars Celebrandi: Celebrating and Concelebrating Mass* (Collegeville, MN: The Liturgical Press, 2021), 117.
4. The following historical examples are identified by Christopher Walsh in 'Concelebration' in *The New SCM Dictionary of Liturgy and Worship*, edited by Paul F Bradshaw (London: SCM Press, 2002), 124-126.

presenting the gifts, over which the presbyters extend hands, whilst the bishop alone prays the prayer of thanks. At about the same time, the *Didascalia* includes reference to a bishop in Syria welcoming a visiting bishop to both preach and to say parts of the eucharistic prayer. Importantly, in this era, there is no question of simultaneous recitation, as liturgical prayers were still improvised.

By the fourth century, Cyril of Jerusalem and Pseudo-Dionysius the Areopagite refer to the celebration of the eucharist presided over by the bishop with his presbyters. Later, the Council of Constantinople (680) and the Synod of Photia (880) note that Latin participants were invited to concelebrate with the Greeks, however, the Latin participants did not know enough Greek to recite the eucharistic prayer.

The eighth century *Ordo Romanus Primus* contains a rubric that directs concelebrating bishops and priests to bow their head during the pope's praying of the eucharistic prayer. In addition, *Ordo III* in Rome orders that the cardinal priests say the eucharistic prayer together with the pope, each holding the bread individually. After the eighth century, so-called 'private Masses' emerged which led to the eventual replacement of the single concelebrated liturgy, although remnants of concelebration survived on Holy Thursday and during the blessing of oils within the eucharistic prayer at that liturgy.

Later, in the twelfth and thirteenth centuries, pontificals— the liturgical book used by the pope—contain references to concelebration during ordinations of bishops and priests. Rubrics from these sources refer to all the concelebrants reciting, *sotto voce*, the prayers from the offertory onwards, and in some cases from the beginning of Mass, including the choir chants of the proper. Also in the thirteenth century, the writings of St Thomas Aquinas (1225–1274) indicate that the practice of concelebration is diminishing. Thomas, however, interprets concelebration as an expression of the unity of the priesthood of Christ. From the sixteenth-century Reformation through to the middle of the twentieth century, the practice of concelebration was confined to the ordination rites for new priests and bishops. The 1917 *Code of Canon Law* (canon 803) affirmed this limitation by restricting concelebration to ordination liturgies.[5]

Clearly, there is an ancient history of concelebration in the Catholic Church; however, our current predicament of large-scale

---

5. See Turner, *Ars Celebrandi*, 120.

concelebration is due to developments that occurred at the Second Vatican Council in the 1960s.

Vatican Council II and the Restoration of Eucharistic Concelebration

Immediately prior to Vatican II, as part of the liturgical movement of the nineteenth and twentieth centuries, there was a call for the restoration of concelebration to deal with the then common practice of 'private Masses' by priests and members of religious orders wishing to observe a commitment to celebrating daily Mass as part of their priestly ministry and identity. The side chapels and altars in historic basilicas, cathedrals, monasteries, abbeys and even parish churches are a clear reflection of this earlier liturgical practice.

Concelebration was introduced into the conciliar discussions relatively early. One practical reason was to address the daily Mass needs of more than 2,000 bishops in Rome for the Council. To assist deliberations, some liturgical experiments were undertaken in various monastic (mostly Benedictine) communities, including Sant'Anselmo in Rome, Maria Laach in Germany and St John's Abbey in the United States.[6]

Archbishop Annibale Bugnini's account of the restoration of concelebration at Vatican II notes that one of the conditions placed upon the experiments in abbeys in 1964 was that there be no more than twenty concelebrants around the altar. Bugnini recounts that in relation to the 1964 Eucharistic Congress in Bombay (now Mumbai), Paul VI approved concelebration with the proviso that the number of concelebrants be limited and that there be someone to serve as master of ceremonies.[7]

Bugnini also notes that in 1965 the Vatican's Congregation of Rites made a series of observations in relation to the proposed definitive Rite of Concelebration. One of the Congregation's chief objections had to do with the number of concelebrants. According to Bugnini, the Consilium's schema suggested that the number of concelebrants be about fifteen. The criterion was 'that all the concelebrants be able to stand around the altar during all their actions and to concelebrate on

---

6. Bugnini, *The Reform of the Liturgy*, 124.
7. Bugnini, *The Reform of the Liturgy*, 125.

it.'⁸ One can locate online archival photos of concelebrated liturgies at the council with concelebrants joining Paul VI literally surrounding the altar on each side inside St Peter's Basilica, a practice which presumably affected visibility by all present. The issue of impaired visibility is still relevant today, particularly when excessive numbers of concelebrants obscure the liturgical focus upon or visibility of the principal celebrant by the people in the main body of the church or assembly.

Bugnini recalls that around the mid-1960s, Paul VI suggested the number of concelebrants be limited to between twenty and twenty-five,⁹ reflecting a fear that a larger number would keep the celebration from proceeding in an orderly and dignified manner. Others outside the Curia and confines of the Vatican urged that the number not be limited. The number fifty took both views into account. The final solution, which reflects current practice, left the number undetermined and simply decreed that 'in each case the number of concelebrants is to be settled by considering how many the church and the altar can accommodate, even if all the concelebrants are not right next to the table of the altar. The faithful's clear view of the rite must be ensured; it is therefore better for the concelebrants not to be stationed between the altar and the people'.¹⁰

Ecclesial Issues: Priestly Unity, Identity and Diversity of Ministries

To understand why concelebration is customary, some ecclesial issues need to be considered. According to the Catholic Church's liturgical documents, eucharistic concelebration helps to manifest the unity of the priesthood along with the hierarchy of ministries in the church.¹¹ This perspective makes sense during ordinations to the priesthood and the episcopacy, which take place within a eucharistic liturgy.

---

8. Bugnini, *The Reform of the Liturgy*, 127.
9. Bugnini, *The Reform of the Liturgy*, 127.
10. SC Rites (Consilium), *Rite of Concelebration*, Introduction, 7 March 1965 (Vatican: Polyglot Press, 1965), 13–18, in *Documents on the Liturgy, 1963–1979: Conciliar, Papal and Curial Texts* (Collegeville, MN: The Liturgical Press, 1982), no. 223, para. 1797, 556–8.
11. Vatican Council II, *Sacrosanctum Concilium* (1963), para. 57, https://www.vatican.va/archive/hist_councils/ii_vatican_council/documents/vat-ii_const_19631204_sacrosanctum-concilium_en.html. Accessed 11 January 2025.

However, at large-scale eucharistic celebrations (such as Masses at plenary councils, national or international eucharistic congresses and international synods), it inevitably means that the processional moments become overly protracted and can end up looking 'cliquey' and clerical, which does not harmonise well with the eucharistic liturgy being a sign of ecclesial unity for *all* present. Optics here are important.

Apart from ecclesial issues, there are also powerful personal preferences of priests to concelebrate, which stems from the desire of many clergy to enact the central aspect of their priestly identity, Eucharist. From another perspective, those with reservations about concelebration in general suggest that the sacrament of orders does not negate one's fundamental baptismal identity in Christ, which is shared with religious and laity, and that giving expression to this primordial sacrament of Christian identity as a member of the assembly can also be viewed as part of a priest's identity.

From the perspective of the clergy, the option to concelebrate is well grounded. Vatican II's Constitution on the Sacred Liturgy, *Sacrosanctum concilium* (1963), the highest level of liturgical law, indicates that concelebration is the required form of celebration not only at ordinations but also at the Chrism Mass and Evening Mass of the Lord's Supper on Holy Thursday, Masses during councils, bishops' conferences and synods and, lastly, the Mass for the blessing of an abbot, plus a few other patronal occasions. The constitution says regulation of concelebration falls to the diocesan bishop.[12]

Twenty years later, the revised *Code of Canon Law* (1983) indicates that a priest is free to concelebrate at Mass.[13] Nevertheless, liturgical law specialist John Huels has pointed out that this canon is not saying that each priest enjoys the automatic *right* to concelebrate.[14] A factor that needs consideration in more recent times, following the Australian Government's Royal Commission into Institutional Responses to Child Sexual Abuse, is that Catholic priests need to provide official paperwork when entering another diocese to

---

12. *Sacrosanctum concilium*, para. 57.
13. Canon 902, *Code of Canon Law* (Washington, DC: Canon Law Society of America, 1983), 338–9, < https://www.vatican.va/archive/cod-iuris-canonici/cic_index_en.html>. Accessed 11 January 2025.
14. John Huels, *Disputed Questions in the Liturgy Today* (Chicago: Liturgy Training Publications, 1988), 43.

indicate that they are a priest in 'good standing' before being officially authorised to concelebrate at Mass.[15]

From a more general point of view, priests cannot be compelled to concelebrate the Eucharist, except in the case of the Mass during which they are ordained. At the same time, the 2011 General Instruction of the Roman Missal (hereafter GIRM), another important source of liturgical norms for Mass, reiterates the conciliar decree on the liturgy by stipulating specific liturgies where concelebration is mandated as the form of celebration: the ordinations of presbyters and bishops, the blessing of an abbot and the Chrism Mass.[16] Again, this rubric does not mean all priests are required to concelebrate, though the liturgy should be a concelebrated one.

What, then, is the general expectation of the church's legislation in relation to priests at a large-scale Mass? GIRM provides the basic norm: 'Concelebration is recommended, unless the good of the Christian faithful requires or suggests otherwise'.[17] The GIRM also says that

> priests who are present at a celebration of the Eucharist, unless excused for a just reason, should usually exercise the function proper to their Order and hence take part as concelebrants, wearing sacred vestments. Otherwise, they wear their proper choir dress (i.e. white surplice over black soutane) or their surplice over a cassock.[18]

Broader Considerations: Synodal Church Context

Having explored some of the historical and ecclesial background to concelebration, let us now explore the synodal context of Catholicism today. Synodality is not a new concept for the Catholic Church; however, the theme has been emphasised during the pontificate of Pope Francis (2013–25), particularly in relation to the synods of bishops. Since 1965, synods of bishops have taken place every three or four years at the Vatican for the bishops to help guide the pope in

---

15. GIRM, para. 200. See General Instruction of the Roman Missal, <https://www.vatican.va/roman_curia/congregations/ccdds/documents/rc_con_ccdds_doc_20030317_ordinamento-messale_en.html>. Accessed 11 January 2025.
16. GIRM, para. 199.
17. GIRM, para. 199.
18. GIRM, para. 114.

his role as universal pastor. The term *synod* comes from the Greek words *syn* (meaning 'together') and *hodos* (meaning 'road' or 'way') and denotes a mode of collaborating along the path of Christian ministry and discipleship.

According to the Vatican website, synodal meetings provide opportunities for the sharing of information and experiences, 'in the common pursuit of pastoral solutions which have a universal validity and application'.[19] The use of the three terms *communion, participation* and *mission* in relation to the recent Vatican Synod for a Synodal Church (October 2023–October 2024) suggests that the synodal process is a way to foster those qualities in the church today.

The pontificate of Francis saw the broadening of synod meetings to include not only bishops but also priests, religious and laity, especially women, as part of the membership. The process included broader opportunities for individual contributions, shared listening, silence, discernment and resolutions voted upon by all synod members. Rather than listening to a series of lectures by bishops, all of them male, Pope Francis' synodal style implied that the usual way of running a synod is not serving the church's needs sufficiently, particularly when half the church's active membership—women—have not been allowed to participate in the synodal process and deliberations, until now.

By implication, another way of looking at eucharistic concelebration within this synodal context is to ask the question: What might the 'good of the Christian faithful' mean in large-scale eucharistic concelebrations? This question is especially relevant in today's modern world with its concerns for peace and justice, promotion of human rights, the equal baptismal dignity of women, men and children, especially the perspective of women who are excluded from ordination to the diaconate and the priesthood. This position is despite the recent work of scholars such as Phyllis Zagano, who has served as member of the pontifical commission examining the diaconate and who argues that there is precedent for the ordination of women to the diaconate in the church's tradition.[20]

---

19. See 'The Synod of Bishops: An Introduction', <https://www.vatican.va/roman_curia/synod/documents/rc_synod_01011995_profile_en.html#:~:text=The%20Synod%2C%20generally%20speaking%2C%20can,Church%20by%20rendering%20their%20counsel>. Accessed 7 January 2025.
20. Phyllis Zagano, editor, *Women Deacons: Essays with Answers* (Collegeville, MN: Michael Glazier, 2016).

Other liturgical scholars such as the late Mary Collins have noted that, sadly, the eucharist as celebrated today is experienced by many women, particularly members of religious orders, as a source of exclusion and alienation in today's church.[21] According to Collins, many women's religious communities turn to Celebrations of the Word with Communion and the Liturgy of the Hours for liturgical celebrations within their own communities so that they can exercise more freely their own baptismal gifts and respond to calls to lead liturgical prayer without calling upon the ministry of priest to preside.

Synodality and Clericalism

Within the synodal context promoted by the late Pope Francis, it seems that all members of the Catholic Church today are being invited to re-examine clerical attitudes and practices amongst clergy and laity that may be counterproductive to the church's witness and its exercise of communion, participation and mission. The most serious example of clericalism, that is, a presumption of self-entitlement by clerics and the legal and moral disregard for adults and children, is sexual abuse of the vulnerable by priests and religious. Clerical practices are not confined to the church, of course, as fraudulent and abusive business and political practices might be regarded as a parallel sense of entitlement. However, the clerical sexual abuse scandal is probably one of the most serious challenges to affect the church since the Reformation.

Writing on the negative influence of clericalism upon the priesthood, American Jesuit priest George Wilson has cited concelebration as an example of a liturgical practice that has produced some mixed results. For example, concelebration does provide a positive focus on the corporate nature of the priesthood. At the same time, concelebration can lead to very divisive and counterproductive situations. Wilson cites the situation where bishops with leaders of male and female religious orders meet in a very inclusive meeting and social context, which is then followed by concelebrated liturgies that effectively undermine the entire gathering and send contradictory

---

21. Mary Collins, 'Is the Eucharist Still a Source of Meaning for Women?' in *Living in the Meantime: Concerning the Transformation of Religious Life,* edited Paul J Philibert, OP (New Jersey: Paulist Press, 1994), 185–196.

messages about collaborative ministry in the church today.[22] The final concelebrated Mass of the recent Synod for a Synodal Church in St Peter's Basilica in Rome was another case in point.

To counter the influence of entitlement amongst the clergy, it is timely to recall Christ's command to do what he did for his followers, to adopt the lower position of servant rather than the position of lord and master (to which Christ was entitled), so that the celebrations of Eucharist can once again become a source of unity, a sacrament of love and service, and an example of ministerial self-gift and self-emptying. The prophetic actions and words of Jesus at the Last Supper, recounted in different ways in each of the gospels, including Jesus' washing the feet of his disciples, suggest the eucharistic ritual needs to be rediscovered and experienced as a source of unity and empowerment rather than privileged entitlement that can create perceptions of division or exclusion.

During a time in the church's history when up to ninety percent of Catholics in many developed countries have given up regular attendance at Sunday Mass, one cannot help but suggest that current approaches to the eucharistic celebration here and elsewhere require serious review. Large-scale concelebration is just one issue; other issues concern the need for ongoing formation in relation to the ministries of preaching, presiding and music.

Large-scale eucharistic concelebrations are, admittedly, relatively rare, but these liturgies are generally broadcast online and reveal the Catholic Church's operative ecclesial definitions of communion, participation and mission, not to mention the human values of inclusion or exclusion within the contemporary church. In terms of sign value, the church's liturgical rites can be described as the public face of the Catholic Church. To paraphrase the ancient axiom *lex orandi, lex credendi*, (and *lex vivendi*), the liturgy as celebrated and ritualised, and not just the official texts, speaks volumes about what the church *actually* believes and lives.

The current concelebratory practices make one wonder whether large-scale liturgies at eucharistic congresses and synods should restrict the number of concelebrants, with the remaining clergy wearing choir dress (as required by GIRM) or alb and stole (familiar

---

22. George Wilson, *Clericalism: The Death of Priesthood* (Collegeville, MN: The Liturgical Press, 2008), 54–55.

symbols of baptism and ordained ministry) and participate from places other than the sanctuary. That alternative style of ministry by the clergy could also be arguably viewed as a form of humble service and discipleship of Christ, who did not claim his equality with God but emptied himself (Phil. 2:6) and assumed the position of a slave (John 13:1-17), serving his disciples rather than presuming to be served.

Synodality and Justice

From another angle, a Synodal Church invites all its members to re-examine customary modes of thinking and acting so the values of justice that Jesus preached and that the church teaches are upheld. Justice is described in the *Catechism of the Catholic Church* as one of the cardinal virtues and a moral virtue. Justice 'disposes one to respect the rights of each and to establish in human relationships the harmony that promotes equity regarding persons and to the common good. The just man [or woman], often mentioned in the Sacred Scriptures, is distinguished by habitual right thinking and the up-rightness of his [or her] conduct toward his [or her] neighbour'.[23] One could infer from this teaching that attitudes and practices within the church's eucharistic liturgy need to be seen to foster justice and harmony between the ministries present, reflecting the mutual love of the persons of the Trinity, the unity within the Body of Christ where all are one, so that as many as possible experience the liturgy as a source of loving, unified and just relationships.

Just Relations between Clergy and Laity

Since the Second Vatican Council, many priests have tried to model increasingly positive and just relations between clergy, religious and laity by fostering the teachings of Vatican II and promoting an inclusive approach to the church's life and ministry. They have often tried to embody this approach by deciding to sit with their parishioners in large-scale celebrations. In the words of one former

---

23. *Catechism of the Catholic Church*, para. 1807 (Strathfield, NSW: St Pauls Publications, 1992), 444. See also <https://www.vatican.va/archive/ENG0015/_INDEX.HTM>. Accessed 11 January 2025.

priest and religious, and a liturgical scholar, the human-spiritual bond of a priest to members of his parish community reflected in his sitting with them at a large-scale Mass is more important than giving expression to his ministerial role in the church.

Noble Simplicity and the Liturgy

Before suggesting some possible alternative strategies to this whole issue, here is a brief comment about the effect of concelebration on noble simplicity and the liturgy. One of the most notable contrasts between the 1962 Tridentine Mass in Latin and the 1969 *Novus Ordo* in the vernacular has been the simplification of the ritual, including minimising duplications and repetitions of words and rituals. This movement recaptures the restraint of the early Roman Rite, which English liturgist Edmund Bishop (1846–1917) claimed was marked by sobriety and moderation.[24]

Given this general trajectory towards simplicity and clarity of style, which helps participants to focus more easily on the liturgical action, it seems incongruous to allow unregulated multiplication of concelebrants in large-scale liturgies, often with clergy who, unwittingly, compete with the main celebrant for attention. One recent example is the image of concelebrating clergy surrounding the new altar at Notre Dame Cathedral in Paris in December 2024.

Admittedly, large-scale Masses do need the services of extra deacons and servers, additional cantors, choir members and instrumentalists, larger numbers of communion ministers, to support the scale of celebration, but one can rightly ask: Does the celebration benefit substantially by increasing the number of concelebrating clergy? Many would answer no! Presumably the needs of individual priests themselves are met, but how are the needs of the faithful met by an additional fifty or more concelebrating clergy? And to those who object that the grandeur of the ceremonial will be compromised, creating a visual spectacle at processional moments can be achieved by the inclusion of other ministers.

---

24. Edmund Bishop, *Liturgica Historica: Papers on the Liturgy and Religious Life of the Western Church* (London: Oxford at the Clarendon Press, 1918), 12.

Possible Strategies

Restore Limits

Following the precedent set by Pope Paul VI, who asked that concelebrants be limited to twenty-five or fewer, organisers of large-scale liturgical celebrations should follow suit, with the approval of the diocesan bishop. More restrictive options might be to limit the numbers of concelebrants to twelve (which calls to mind the twelve apostles at the Last Supper), though this limitation might trouble some people on the grounds of appearing to be too literal. Gil Ostdiek has indicated that smaller numbers might also encourage a form of elitism about who is chosen and who is not chosen to concelebrate.[25]

A still further restriction might be to limit the number of concelebrants to zero but to provide two deacons either side of the main celebrant so that there are three ministers at the altar during the eucharistic prayer and one either side of the presiding celebrant at other times. This would give due prominence to the presidential and diaconal aspects of the eucharistic celebration and provide some continuity with the Tridentine high Mass, which was led by a priest, deacon, and subdeacon only, with other clergy assisting 'in choir'.

Ministers of Holy Communion

Clearly, sufficient ministers of holy communion need to be provided at large-scale liturgies to facilitate the distribution of communion to members of the assembly. If large numbers of priests and deacons are present and are vested in choir dress or alb and stole, there does not appear to be any reason to prevent their distribution of communion, assisted by lay extraordinary ministers, also vested, where possible.

A set of identical stoles could be provided for clergy, and would be, in fact, easier and more economical to provide than a set of identical chasubles for concelebrants. Vested clergy, modelling the example of Christ's hospitality towards his disciples at the Last Supper, could take up positions within the assembly that facilitates their ministry at communion but not routinely be involved in entrance and concluding processions. After all, taking a lesser seat is part of the Christ-centred

---

25. See Gilbert Ostdiek, 'Concelebration Revisited' in *Shaping English Liturgy*, edited by Peter Finn and James Schellman (Washington, DC: The Pastoral Press, 1990), 139–71; here n. 88

way of life (Lk 14:10) and something the baptised do within churches each week.

Christ's example of washing his disciple's feet at the Last Supper suggests that disciples of Christ today, whether they be bishops, clergy, religious or lay faithful, should emulate their master's example in humble service of others, particularly during the eucharistic ritual which Christ asked his followers to continue in his memory. Rather than presuming to concelebrate, priests could undertake related ministries such welcoming people and ministering communion, which they are used to doing already.

Conclusion

Returning to the question of the appropriateness in the Synodal Church context of eucharistic concelebration, it should be clear that the practice of concelebration should be limited in large-scale eucharistic celebrations, primarily to limit perceptions of clericalism and to avoid the potential for ritual and ministerial distortions. The Second Vatican Council's reform of the liturgy was primarily designed to foster the full, conscious and active participation of the faithful in the church's liturgical prayer. In our modern age, in which our secular culture is shining a spotlight for the church highlighting the importance of equal opportunities for women and men in many workplace and service roles, the Catholic Church should be a beacon of light illustrating how the theological goals of communion, participation and mission can be practiced with increased credibility for sceptical members of the church and the wider culture today.

In the church's largest-scale liturgies at local, national and international levels, remembering that these liturgies are normally broadcast and reveal the operating definitions of the Eucharist and church as a sacrament of unity, the Catholic Church needs to model 'best practice' in fidelity to the Lord's commands, and the church's long and varied traditions, so that the Eucharist will be experienced increasingly by all the faithful as a compelling expression of unity, and model a deepened awareness of justice at the heart of the liturgy.

Clanging Symbols: Gender and Ordination in the Lutheran Church of Australia and New Zealand

Michelle Eastwood

Michelle Eastwood is Director of Research at Australian Lutheran College. Her research interests include Hebrew Bible, gender and sexuality, public theology, and worship and liturgy within the gathered community. Michelle is co-editor of *Reading the Bible in Australia* (Wipf and Stock, 2024) and *Modern Liturgies for Australia* (Garrat Publications, 2025). She lives, works and plays on the unceded land of the Wadawurrung People.

Abstract

Within church practice, gender can be understood as a symbol that illustrates inequality, communicating hierarchical interpretations of worthiness and ability. This applies to the issue of ordination, which is often representative of male normativity within churches and church practices. The Lutheran Church of Australia and New Zealand (LCANZ) has recently experienced a schism over the decision to ordain women as well as men. This decision has been over forty years in the making, with theological and biblical justifications and arguments traded from both sides. This paper explores the ways that gender has become a clanging symbol within the LCANZ and within liturgical practice more broadly.

'If I speak in the tongues of humans and of angels but do not have love, I am a noisy gong or a clanging cymbal'.[1] So said Paul in the First

---

1. All Bible quotes are drawn from the NRSVUE unless otherwise indicated.

Letter to the Corinthians (13:1). This is not a new issue for the people of God, reflecting similar issues that are raised in prophetic books such as Isaiah (1:10–15; 29:13), as well as in current debates within and between different Christian denominations. Right worship requires right relationships.

The Lutheran Church of Australia and New Zealand has recently experienced a schism because of the synod decision in October 2024 to ordain women as well as men. This decision has been over forty years in the making, with theological and biblical justifications and arguments being traded from both sides. It has caused splits in families, friends and church communities, who have found themselves on opposing sides of this issue.

This paper will consider the rhetoric and symbolism that has been used throughout this debate and the impact that it has had on various parties, particularly the symbolic nature of gender and its limitations. This paper is situated generally in the field of semiotics—the study of signs and symbols and their use or interpretation. The clanging cymbal that Paul references in the verse above, with a presumably loud and discordant sound, provides an excellent metaphor for the way symbols, including gender, can be received as unpleasant and cacophonous in worship.

Worship in this paper is broadly conceived as a place where participants engage in communal and theological meaning-making. Because worship is always contextual, I note that my perspective is informed by Protestant traditions, and I am writing generally from that perspective, having spent many years worshipping in Lutheran, Anglican and Uniting Church contexts. In this vein, I argue that gender within the church has become, or perhaps has always been, a clanging symbol that is representative of hierarchical relationships within the ecclesial body that undermines the command to love one another as oneself. Gender can be understood as a symbol because, as Judith Butler has argued, it is inherently social, contextual, and performative rather than being linked to any physical reality.[2]

A hierarchical understanding of gender is of course, not limited to the church. It has long been understood that we live in a patriarchal

---

2. See Judith P Butler, *Gender Trouble: Feminism and the Subversion of Identity* (Milton Park, UK: Routledge Classics, [1990] 2006).

society, and that patriarchies have been the dominate form of society, at least since the age of empire and the growth of nation-states.[3] However, as broader society has become more aware of the negative impacts for both men and women that patriarchy encourages, the continuing defence of gender inequality in the church on theological grounds leads to growing numbers of people disaffiliating, contributing to declining church attendance and decreased individual identification with Christianity. Thus it may be understood as a clanging symbol.[4]

One clear symbol of gendered hierarchies in the church is the issue of the ordination of women. The fact that the ordination of men is normative while the ordination of women is an 'issue' demonstrates the inherent inequality connected to this practise. The inherent link between ordination and authorised worship practices means that, when individuals are denied the ability to preside because of their gender, it becomes an outsized symbol of general inequality within the church. This is particularly true for churches that prioritise liturgical practise as a key part of their identity, such as the Lutheran Church of Australia and New Zealand.

---

3. Angela Saini outlines the historical evidence for patriarchal and non-patriarchal societies demonstrating that patriarchy is not inevitable. See Angela Saini, *The Patriarch: How Men Came to Rule* (San Francisco: HarperCollins Publishers, 2024).
4. Rosie Clare Shorter and Tanay Riches note that the discrepancy in leadership positions by gender and the failures around financial and sexual misconduct are linked to women's declining attendance within Pentecostalism in Australia. See Rosie Clare Shorter and Tanya Riches, 'We're Told Pentecostal Churches like Hillsong Are Growing in Australia, but They're Not Anymore—Is There a Gender Problem?' *The Conversation*, 27 February 2023, <https://theconversation.com/were-told-pentecostal-churches-like-hillsong-are-growing-in-australia-but-theyre-not-anymore-is-there-a-gender-problem-199413>. Accessed 11 November 2025. Tracy McEwan demonstrates that declining religiosity for women within the Catholic Church is attributable to a range of factors and is not consistent across generational cohorts. See Tracy McEwan, 'Changing Patterns of Religious Practice and Belief among Church-attending Catholic Women in Australia', JASR 31/3 (2018): 186–215, <https://doi.org/10.1558/jasr.37574>. Philip Hughes notes that there has been a connection made between changing values including gendered expectations, moral failures and the issue of sexual abuse within the church, and church attendance but reports that this is not distinguished by gender. Philip Hughes, 'Why People Are Ceasing to Attend Churches and to Identify with Religious Institutions', *Journal of Contemporary Ministry*, 9 (2024): 101–49.

Gender and Ordination in the Lutheran Church in Australia and New Zealand

The Lutheran Church of Australia and New Zealand at its General Synod in October 2024 voted to allow women to be ordained for the first time in its history.[5] The LCA has been one of the most theologically conservative Lutheran churches around the world, with many others having ordained women for decades, including in Germany, the home of Luther and Lutheranism.[6] The vote to ordain women was defined as a doctrinal issue and so required a supermajority—two-thirds of the synod to vote in favour—for it to be accepted. This issue has been presented regularly to the General Synod for the last forty years and has often achieved a majority vote but not the supermajority required for change. In previous years it has come heartbreakingly close, defeated by only a handful of votes.[7]

---

5. Elise Mattiske, 'Synod Enables Ordination of Women and Men', Lutheran Church of Australia, 15 October 2024, <https://www.lca.org.au/synod-enables-ordination-of-women-and-men/>. 11 November 2025.
6. The US-based Lutheran Church–Missouri Synod (LCMS) is one of the key Lutheran Churches that objects to the ordination of women, and it has been influential in encouraging other churches to follow the same doctrinal path. John Koch notes the strong and consistent influence of LCMS in Australia, which included training of ministers who have disproportionate power over doctrinal decisions in Australia. See John B Koch, 'Lutheran Church–Missouri Synod-Trained Pastors and Their Impact on Australian Lutheranism', *Journal of Friends of Lutheran Archives*, 13 (2003): 60–85, <https://search.informit.org/doi/10.3316/ielapa.200400713>. A. Nuernberger reports that, while the practice of women working within 'the institutionalised ministry of the church' has been ongoing since the seventeenth century, the ordination of women within the Lutheran *Landeskirchen* was implemented between 1965 and 1975. See A. Nuernberger (2022), 'Female Ordination: Biblical, Confessional and Hermeneutical Perspectives', *Lutheran Theological Journal*, 56/3 (2022): 155–167. Not all German churches ordain women, however, with the Independent Evangelical Lutheran Church (SELK) recently voting to reject women's ordination even though they have been debating this issue for many years. See Matthew Block, 'Selk Pastoral Convention Offers Clarity on Ordination', International Lutheran Council, 2025, <https://ilcouncil.org/2025/08/14/selk-pastoral-convention-offers-clarity-on-ordination>. Accessed 14 October 2025.
7. In 2015, 64 percent of delegates voted in favour of women's ordination, just 2 percent short of the needed supermajority. See 'Ordination – What's Next?', Lutheran Church of Australia, 20 June 2016, <https://www.lca.org.au/blog/2016/06/20/ordination-whats-next/>. Accessed 11 November 2025.

The LCA, in good Lutheran tradition, believes theoretically in *sola scriptura* as a framework for developing doctrinal understandings. The argument against the ordination of women rests on two main passages: 1 Timothy 2:11–12 and 1 Corinthians 14:33b–38. A 'plain' reading of these two texts can be understood as restricting women from speaking in church rooted in a creation justification that understands Eve as subject to Adam and women in general as more vulnerable to deception than men. However, there have been many words written that suggests these 'plain' readings are inadequate for a range of reasons.[8] I am not going to argue the nuances of these texts here, suffice it to say that I do not think these verses present enough justification to prevent women from being ordained.

The vote has led to a schism between those claiming to be 'confessional' Lutherans, who have named themselves Lutheran Mission–Australia, and the rest of the church. Lutheran Mission–Australia claims an orthodoxy that maintains the 'true spirit' of the Theses of Agreement, the Book of Concord, Luther's Small and Large Catechism, and the Bible. The Theses of Agreement is an agreement constituted in 1966 between the two largest Lutheran synods at the time, the Evangelical Lutheran Church of Australia and the United Evangelical Lutheran Church of Australia, known colloquially as ELCA and UELCA, who joined to create the current LCA.[9] A change to this agreement removing references to male-only clergy was the change approved at the latest synod vote.

Since German immigrants arrived in these lands now called Australia, there have always been multiple Lutheran churches.[10] The LCA website states that 'in the early 1900s, there were eight separate Lutheran churches, plus some independent Lutheran pastors'.

---

8. Biblical scholar Marg Mowczko has written on these passages numerous times providing a general introduction to the issues involved in both passages, including Marg Mowczko, 'Six Reasons 1 Timothy 2:12 Is Not as Clear as It Seems', 3 August 2016, <https://margmowczko.com/1-timothy-212-not-as-clear>; and 'The Chiasm in 1 Corinthians 11:2–16', 19 November 2012, <https://margmowczko.com/the-chiasm-in-1-corinthians-11_2-16>. Accessed 14 October 2025.
9. Lutheran Church of Australia, 'Foundational Documents—Lutheran Church of Australia', 8 June 8, 2024, <https://www.lca.org.au/foundational-documents>. Accessed 14 October 2025.
10. A diagrammatical representation of the different synods can be found at: <https://www.lca.org.au/our-history>, under the heading 'Division and Unity'. Accessed 14 October 2025.

Lutherans in Australia (and possibly around the world) have a long history of schism and reconciliation. While this observation might also be true of other denominations, I think in terms of the Lutheran churches there are some observable traits that make schism more likely.

First, a focus on purity within doctrine and worship leads those having different understandings to part ways. The Lutheran church itself, of course came into existence because of a schism from the Roman church, over the issue of indulgences among other things. The early Lutherans came to Australia also because of a schism. Friederick William III of Prussia (himself a Reformed Protestant) enacted a union between the Reformed and Lutheran churches in Prussia, which included among other things a shared common prayer book and liturgy. For many Lutherans, the differences between the Lutheran and Reformed churches were not significant and could be dealt with in good faith. However, there were some such as August Kavel, Gotthard Fritzsche and others who found the union unconscionable. At great personal cost, they travelled with members of their congregations across the oceans to start a new life,[11] some to South Australia, but others to the United States and Canada. The insistence on right worship, right doctrine, and right belief was a founding principle for Australian Lutherans, and these 'purity impulses' (as I would name them) have continued to inform the practices of Lutherans in Australia ever since.

A second trait is the priority placed on the biblical texts. As noted, Lutherans ostensibly hold to *sola scriptura*, which informs doctrine, liturgical observance, and church practise. I say ostensibly because as noted, even those Lutherans who proclaim that they are the only faithful observers of orthodoxy hold to a range of post-biblical texts, with the justification that these contain a 'faithful exposition' of the scriptures. While the Bible is held in greater esteem than any of these other texts, they are certainly drawn upon to add justification and sometimes clarification when the Bible is not sufficiently clear on a given issue.

---

11. Everard Leske details the history and costs involved in *For Faith and Freedom: The Story of Lutherans and Lutheranism in Australia 1838-1996* (Cambridge: Openbook Publishers, 1996).

Just as the anti-women's ordination movement uses scripture to justify their position, so too has the pro-women's ordination movement.[12] The examples of Junia, Priscilla, Mary Magdalene, and other women leaders in the Bible demonstrate the role of women even within the earliest Jesus movement, alongside passages such as Galatians 3:28, which reject social divisions that were commonly accepted at the time. This use of the Bible as the primary justification or opposition to women's ordination can be seen as distinct from other denominations and traditions with respect to the rhetoric around the issue of ordination, which prioritise the argument that Jesus was a man, and therefore only men can act *in persona Christi*, and that the twelve disciples were men and therefore male-only leadership is divinely approved. These arguments have been present in the LCA but are often considered secondary.

The biblical arguments for and against women's ordination have been rehearsed within and without the LCA for decades. They often sound more like a *post hoc* analysis that seeks to justify a pre-existing position rather than an objective or impartial exploration of the text. This is not to say that the biblical witness is unimportant. As a biblical scholar, this is obviously not a position I hold. Rather, I argue that the Bible must be read as an ancient document that is responding to its own social and cultural contexts and must be read with these situations in mind. The biblical writers are clear on their acceptance of—if not outright support for—slavery, and yet there are no contemporary voices that I know that would support slavery. But this was not true in the nineteenth century, when the abolition movement was at its zenith, or even in the last century when similar arguments were made to support apartheid in South Africa. We have come to understand that it is not moral to own another person, even if it is in the Bible.

Nevertheless, the Bible continues to be used to insist on hierarchical gender norms which include but go well beyond the issue of ordination. Gender norms, in the church as in wider society, are so ingrained as to seem almost natural. In fact, many of the current arguments for upholding gender norms and hierarchies are rooted in the idea that gender is a biological phenomenon and that a gender binary is the natural, traditional and biblical form that has

---

12. See: Noel C Shultz, *Neither Male nor Female* (Bayswater: Coventry Press, 2020).

been undermined in contemporary society by feminist and queer activists who are pushing their own (secular) agenda. Often unsaid within this pre-supposition is that the agenda is to take power away from the hands of cis-gender straight white men and place it into the hands of women, non-white and queer people. The power of white men is assumed to be natural and right, while all others are seen as power hungry, overly ambitious, and usurping the natural order. These assumptions are often unarticulated but emerge in comments, rhetoric and spurious correlations. Therefore, if we recognise that gendered hierarchies are also, like slavery, immoral, then it behoves us to let them go too. But this is perhaps the crux of the issue.

Making Meaning from the 'Clang'

The field of semiotics and its focus on how symbols function beyond articulated understandings can help to explore issues including normative gendered hierarchies. In *Worship as Meaning: A Liturgical Theology for Late Modernity*, Graham Hughes argues that a constant factor in worship is that 'people are attempting to offer a meaningful account of the world, of God, of our human condition'.[13] The worship event is deeply imbued with symbols, signs and meanings that ideally allow the worship participant, whether leader or congregant, to meaningfully experience and encounter the divine.

In a forthcoming chapter titled 'What Are You Wearing? The Signification of Liturgical Dress on Social Media', I note that

> Liturgical robes do not have any inherent meaning. Rather their meaning is derived from the situation in which they are worn. In worship, the role of the presider is to facilitate the ritual actions which constitute the service. Liturgical robes in this context serve as a symbol which aims to obscure the identity of the presider, in order that participants are able to focus their attention wholly on God.[14]

---

13. Graham Hughes, *Worship as Meaning: A Liturgical Theology for Late Modernity* (Cambridge University Press, 2003), 14.
14. Michelle Eastwood, 'What Are You Wearing? The Signification of Liturgical Dress on Social Media' in *Clerical Dress: Contested Histories from Paul to the Present*, edited by Miles Pattenden and Stephen C Carlson (Leiden, Netherlands: Brill, forthcoming).

In that research I was looking at the connection between liturgical robes and identity, namely through the construction of identity within a Facebook profile picture. Several of the women I interviewed in that research noted the way robes interacted with gender in terms of their clerical identity. One participant noted 'I come across more [gender issues] when I'm not robed'. And another noted that the robes helped identify her as the leader because

> if they don't know me, they're kind of looking around trying to work out who's going to be taking the service, which is what used to happen when I was ordained in the Church of Christ because I just turned up in a suit.

One woman told me that when she is not robed and turns up to ecumenical meetings with her male colleague, he is assumed to be ordained and she is not. This is sadly reminiscent of the many stories we hear about women bosses being assumed to be the secretary when meeting people for the first time in a work situation.

Another woman commented that she wore the robes or a clerical collar in Sydney Anglican circles to be deliberately provocative. She did it for the women who would see her and know that women's ordination was a possibility, because the Sydney Anglican diocese is infamous for its objections to women's ordination as priests in contrast to other Anglican dioceses across Australia. Coincidentally, one Anglican woman told me the story of seeing a woman participate in the entrance procession and the way it inspired her.

> I can still see the image of her. And she's in the procession. She goes past me up into the sanctuary and a voice in my head said, it really is okay to be [ordained]. I wish, I mean, I'm still a bit shocked because that tells me the message I had been getting all my life was that it wasn't. Yeah, that there was something deficient about being a woman. Yeah, processions have been legitimating. And when I saw that, just a light bulb went on.

Every woman that I interviewed mentioned the relationship of their gender to the wearing of liturgical robes, while none of the men did. While this cohort of interviewees was relatively small, and certainly not statistically representative, this data reinforces the stories I have been told casually by female clergy and my own personal experiences in preaching and leading worship. In contrast, I have only met one man who engaged meaningfully with this topic in terms of his own practise. His wife was also ordained, and it was his vicarious experience of discrimination directed toward her that impacted his relationship with the clothes he wore to lead worship. As noted, liturgical robes are meant to obscure the identity of the wearer to encourage focus on the divine, but this research has demonstrated that women often felt like they had to obscure a specific part of their identity—namely their gender—through the use of robes to gain legitimacy in the role of clergy.

It is worth mentioning that gender was not the only symbol connected to wearing liturgical robes that emerged in this research. Robing and clerical attire was connected to a wide range of symbolism: the community of baptism; academic robes; a sign of unity; and power and authority. As I note in my research:

> I have been reminded that there is a beauty in liturgical robes and a symbolism which remains deeply meaningful. However, I have also been conscious that when power and authority have been abused, and church teachings used to belittle, harm or reject people, then the symbolism becomes tainted. The notion that the church has traumatised people was evident in a number of the interviews, and that this trauma could be triggered by seeing liturgical robes or clerical wear was clearly a concern for particular participants.[15]

This serves as a reminder that there are a range of symbols within worship and liturgical practices that may or may not be communicating the intended meanings. An awareness of the range of things these symbols are communicating is invaluable, particularly because of the overtones of divine authority and legitimacy with which these symbols are imbued. This unintentional messaging can only be accessed by asking participants what their understanding of the symbolism is, in sensitive and appropriate ways that avoid demand characteristics which may be present if the questions are asked within spaces that invoke clerical or institutional power dynamics.

---

15. Eastwood, 'What Are You Wearing'.

I am using 'symbol' here in the tradition of CS Pierce, who described it as

> a sign which depends neither on a perceived similarity between the sign's vehicle and its object, nor on mechanical causation, but simply on the fact that it has become conventional to see one thing as a sign of something else.[16]

In this discussion, gender identity is the object which can be understood as female, male or queer or non-binary identity, and which carries a range of meanings unconnected to the actual physicality of one's biological form, being the vehicle. Gender identity carries with it a range of signifiers. For example, it has become conventional to see woman or femaleness as a sign of submission, femininity, weakness, and modesty, as well as being disruptive, emotional, irrational, and seductive, even though there is nothing inherent about a female body that is connected to these or any other personality traits[17] (or to a male body for that matter). Judith Butler reminds us that if these associations were natural, then there would be no need to reinforce or police them.[18]

These associations and symbolism are not naturally occurring. The association between the vehicle and its object are socially constructed by what Pierce calls an *interpretant*. Hughes explains, 'It is the interpretant which mediates between the sign's vehicle and object thus generating the signification found therein.'[19] The interpretant does not make meaning alone; each interpretant or individual makes meaning from within their own social and cultural location which carry dominant narratives about the way the world is. So, understandings about the meaning of gender are rooted in wider cultural conceptions and are reinforced through social interactions from when a child is born through to old age.

In the last twenty years, understandings of gender within Australia and other Western nations have undergone a distinct change to

---

16. Quoted in Hughes, *Worship as Meaning*, 141.
17. These issues have been explored at length by Angela Saini, *Inferior: How Science Got Women Wrong and the New Research That's Rewriting the Story* (London: Fourth Estate, 2017); and Cordelia Fine, *Delusions of Gender: How Our Minds, Society, and Neurosexism Create Difference* (London: Icon Books, 2010).
18. See Butler, *Gender Trouble*, 2–3.
19. Hughes, *Meaning in Worship*, 142.

include non-binary and queer presentations that are understood via notions of performativity and identity rather than an assumed biological reality. Within non-Western traditions there is a long history of non-binary presentations of gender, as well as the reference to eunuchs in Matthew 19, which suggest that gender has always been understood as more than binary. The progress towards a more diverse understanding of gender and gender identity, has been met with a backlash claiming that a hierarchical gender binary is derived from a natural order, which is often reinforced through particular readings of biblical texts. The hierarchical nature of gender is reinforced within ecclesial and liturgical spaces through a range of symbolisms.

It is more than thirty years since the publication of Elizabeth Johnson's *She Who Is,* which explored conceptualisations of the divine as male within theological and liturgical language and how this promotes patriarchal practices within the church.[20] It is over fifty years since Mary Daly noted that 'if God is male, the male is God'.[21] The problematic nature of gendering God as exclusively male has long been acknowledged and this has led to moves towards inclusive language within some Bible translations and liturgical praxis. However, it is only in some, and my experience even in the Uniting Church of Australia—which is arguably the most progressive of the larger denominations—is that God is still uncritically and regularly addressed primarily as male, including the use of titles such as 'king' and 'lord', and the pronoun 'he'. Another example is that despite their being a range of gender-neutral alternatives, the prayer that Jesus taught is still referred to as the 'Our Father' or 'Lord's Prayer'.

The use of male God-language and its relationship to our perception of human males reinforces an implicit understanding that males have a divinely ordained authority and a natural capacity for leadership. Naturalness is itself a construct and comes with connotations of purity, goodness, and right order, which often arises out of creation ontologies. These often-implicit ontologies can make us feel uncomfortable when boundaries are crossed. For example, if God is speaking within the liturgy, and we are uncomfortable with God being imaged as female, it makes sense that we would feel uncomfortable with a woman leading.

---

20. Elizabeth Johnson, *She Who Is: The Mystery of God in Feminist Theological Discourse* (New York: Crossroad, 1992).
21. Mary Daly, *Beyond God the Father* (Boston: Beacon Press, 1973), 19.

The Bible is undeniably a patriarchal text with more men named in Genesis than there are women across the whole Bible, but the lectionary increases this androcentric bias with the ratio of male–female dominant stories higher in the lectionary than in the Bible itself.[22] Another way that gender emerges is within biblical metaphors such as the marriage motif, which is present across both the Hebrew Bible and the New Testament texts. The marriage metaphor often communicates that the groom is in charge, he chooses his bride, and he is responsible for looking after her. The groom is the stronger party and in texts like Hosea is responsible for chastising and controlling his bride, even to the point of what we would name today as domestic violence. This motif reinforces heteronormative notions of marriage which naturalise hierarchies within male-female gendered relationships.

These understandings are then applied to leadership within the church—as seen in the issue of women's ordination—but is also applicable more widely, including within the appointment of deacons, church council members and other leadership positions. Even when women ordained within a given denomination, their suitability to be clergy is often questioned and undermined. This often does not come from the leadership or in official documents but often happens in informal situations and off-the-cuff comments after the service. Women are less likely to hold full-time ministry positions and are much less likely to be the lead pastor in teams with multiple clergy.[23] As noted in my earlier research, women found that robes and clerical collars seemed to legitimate their position by obscuring their gender,

---

22. Susanne Sartor Ferris, 'The Bible on Steroids: The Effect of Androcentrism on the Lectionary,' *New Theology Review,* 15/1 (2002): 21–31.
23. NCLS data report that while women are over-represented in local church life in every age, they are more likely to have roles that incorporate pastoral care and children's ministry, and less likely to have roles in teaching/preaching and governance. See NCLS.org.au, 'Women's Participation in Church Life and Leadership—NCLS Research', 2021, <https://www.ncls.org.au/articles/womens-participation-in-church-life-and-leadership/>. Accessed 14 October 2025. Within Protestant churches in Australia, only the Salvation Army had a majority of female senior leaders (53.1 percent), while the LCA reported 8.4 percent, possibly reflecting women's leadership in Lutheran schools. See NCLS.org.au, 'Women in Senior Leadership in Their Local Church—NCLS Research', 2021, <https://www.ncls.org.au/articles/women-in-senior-leadership-in-their-local-church/>. Accessed 14 October 2025.

suggesting that the symbolism of the liturgical wear was more salient in those moments than their gender.

When a person is gendered as female, there are a range of expectations she is required to meet including that she is likeable.[24] Liking a woman is often a requirement for respecting her authority, approving of the music or art she creates, or seeing her as a believable victim of crime or unfortunate circumstances. These assessments come from both women and men and apply anytime a woman steps outside of the boundaries deemed as socially acceptable. Of course, people in leadership often need to make difficult decisions, and as soon as a female leader makes these calls, she can be deemed unlikeable. Failure to make the calls may mean she is not considered tough enough to do the job, making them means she is unlikeable. For women, this is a Catch-22 situation

Steps Toward Harmony?

If the clanging symbol of gender is to be addressed, one of the first things is to recognise that it is an issue. One simple way I do this is by counting male instances of God-language in the liturgy. Counting the number of instances of 'lord', 'king', and 'he', whether in prayers, readings, sermons or songs, can be a startling reminder about how male-centric worship continues to be.

Second, we can agitate for change within our own churches on both the local and the national levels. The success of the vote to ordain women in the LCA was the culmination of years of prayer, theological reflection, and coordinated activism that demonstrated over many years that a majority in the church were in favour of women's ordination. Ultimately, the LCA developed a 'one church, two understandings' framework for ordination, similar to the Uniting Church's position on marriage. This means that some in the LCA will continue to teach and preach that male-only ordination is the correct doctrinal and theological position. There will be congregations that choose only to consider male candidates, and there will be people who might change churches if their current church chooses a female minister. This decision does not mean that gender will cease to

---

24. Gloria J Romero, *Just Not That Likeable: The Price All Women Pay for Gender Bias* (Brentwood, TN: PostHill Press, 2021).

be a clanging symbol for many women in the church, but it does demonstrate that part of the issue has been recognised and addressed.

There will also be space in the LCA for the women I know and love—and some I don't know, I'm sure—to answer the call into ordained ministry. There will be congregations who are able to choose to have a female minister. And little girls will be able to see themselves represented as leaders within the worship setting.

While the world is making strides toward gender equality, or at the very least toward an acceptance that gendered inequality is a bad thing, the insistence within the church that gendered inequality is divinely ordained and part of the natural order sends a larger message that the church (and by proxy the Christian God) believes some people are more worthy than others—or perhaps in the heritage of George Orwell's *Animal Farm*—some are more equal than others, purely based on the body they were born into. As long as women are told that they are naturally more caring than men but are kept out of paid pastoral positions; as long as women hold leadership positions in secular society but must submit to men in the church and are not allowed to hold the clerical office in ecclesial communities; as long as women are still told their bodies are a temptation while men are excused from taking responsibility for abuse, gender becomes the clanging symbol warning women that they are not safe and not valued in churches.

Liturgy as a site of meaning-making has the potential to upend traditional understandings that limit women's participation and in turn their perceived worth to the church. It offers the opportunity to teach that power and authority are not situated within one form of the human body, and the responsibility to proclaim that a faithful exposition of the biblical text requires us to critically evaluate scripture through the greatest commandment: to love God and to love neighbour as oneself. Reading the Bible in a way that diminishes another, whether they be female, Indigenous, non-white, queer or any other marginalised identity is simply not loving.

Gender carries a range of symbolisms within and without the church, many of which are implicitly held and largely unrecognised, let alone interrogated. The steps toward ordaining women within the Lutheran Church of Australia is a movement in the right direction, but if the women who are ordained are subject to these implicitly negative evaluations, then they will be at risk of harm and burnout, even more so than at the alarming current average rate for clergy. There are people within the LCA who recognise this, and one of the things that was done in preparation for the ordination of women was research looking at the barriers faced by the first women in other denominations to be ordained, and the ongoing issues women face in ministry.

The motto of the Lutheran Church of Australia is 'where love comes to life,' and having observed this process particularly over the last four years while I have been employed at the Australian Lutheran College, I am more hopeful than ever that gender and women's natural embodied existence may one day cease to be an obstacle to leadership, inclusion and full participation in liturgical practice and everyday church life. Until that day, there continues to be work to do, and I invite you to join with me in the struggle.

Glory and Justice in Christian Living and Worship

Jenny Close

Jenny Close lives in Brisbane and is a recently retired teacher. Her first degree was in fine arts (painting), and then she trained as a teacher, working between secondary school teaching for Brisbane Catholic Education (BCE) and freelance liturgical art making. She was later employed by BCE to work in multimedia video, animation and book illustration. In 2005 she was awarded a PhD from Griffith University for her thesis *A Feminist Understanding of Liturgical Art.* Since 2005, she has worked as a sessional lecturer in theology at Australian Catholic University and Broken Bay Institute, while maintaining her art practice, which has become more digital over the years.

Abstract

In Christian life, praise and justice are two distinct but interrelated aspects of our relationship with God: Our faith life requires that we love God (praise) and do God's work in the world (justice). Ideally, liturgy draws together both these aspects of Christian life. This paper is part of my larger project exploring various aspects of a theology of God and beauty. That project is underpinned by an approach to theological aesthetics which is critical of traditional understandings of beauty. The notion of 'glory' is part of the framework of traditional concepts which I call beauty theology. The traditional focus of theological aesthetics is heavily on the side of glory, but I would argue that a more balanced approach takes justice into account. In this paper I will explore the scriptural and liturgical aspects of both glory and justice.

Introduction

Early in December 2024, I attended an Advent reflection hosted by Women and the Australian Church (WATAC). The meeting began with a reflection on a scripture passage from Baruch (5:1–9), which was the second reading for the Second Sunday of Advent. Baruch directed Jerusalem to '[t]ake off the garment of your sorrow and affliction . . . and put on for ever the beauty of the glory from God' (5:1). The prophet named Jerusalem as the 'peace of righteousness and glory of godliness' (5:4).

I had just recently begun thinking about the nature of the glory of God, so my first reaction was: 'Wow, here is a reading right on my topic—let me take notes!' However, others in the gathering did not miss the elephant in the room. They read this passage in the light of the war in Gaza and struggled to use it for prayer. I agreed with them that, no matter what your politics are, it was difficult to see Israel in terms of righteous peace and godly glory in this context. Glory and justice appear to be very far apart in this real-life situation, and it seems inappropriate to wax lyrical about liturgical matters without considering these morally ambiguous events. Elizabeth Harrington reinforces this point:

> The community that gathers to celebrate the eucharist cannot hear the word of God and share the eucharistic bread and cup without reflecting on what it means to live as a Christian in a world where millions go hungry every day. Breaking bread together must lead us to question a social order in which the gap between rich and poor is growing wider, and which permits bread to be so readily available to some and not to others.[1]

As Christians, justice is at the heart of liturgy. Outreach to the disadvantaged is central to our mission and our liturgical experience is meant to nourish us for this mission. Harrington pointed to a few useful scripture passages, and this one from Amos was particularly evocative:

---

1. Elizabeth Harrington, 'Liturgy and Social Justice', *Liturgy Brisbane,* Liturgy Lines, 28 September 2003, <www.liturgybrisbane.net.au/resources/liturgy-lines/liturgy-and-social-justice/>. Accessed 6 December 2024.

Take away from me the noise of your songs;
I will not listen to the melody of your harps.
But let justice roll down like waters,
and righteousness like an ever-flowing stream (5:23–24).

Here is the problem: There can be a serious disconnect between glory and justice, that is, between what we celebrate and how we live our lives. Moreover, our lived experience teaches us that the glorious ideals and practices of our faith-life must be tested out in the challenges that everyday life throws our way, especially regarding living justly.

So far it seems that I have aligned 'glory' with liturgy and 'justice' with life, and there is some truth to that, but ultimately that is not how it works. The trusted old maxim *lex orandi, lex credendi, lex vivendi* indicates that our liturgical expressions will shape the way we understand who God is, which will in turn shape the way we live our lives. However, to live up to this maxim, glory and justice need to be reconciled across liturgy and life. So, in what follows I will try to show the relationship between these concepts.

Justice

A thorough study of justice would require some deep diving into moral theology, but this is not my area of expertise and such a study would be outside the scope of this article. However, I will point to a reliable source on this topic.

In one of his audiences, Pope Francis expressed some sound ideas on the nature of justice.[2] Francis identified justice as '[t]he constant and firm will to give their due to God and neighbour'. Clearly this is a reference to the greatest commandment in Matthew, chapter 22, and to Luke, chapter 10, the latter of which includes the parable of the Good Samaritan and its perennial question: Who is our neighbour?

Francis comments that '[j]ustice is a virtue for the good coexistence of people'. He cites 'ancient masters' who describe justice in terms of a cluster of virtues: 'benevolence, respect, gratitude, affability, and

---

2. Pope Francis, *General Audience*, Wednesday, 3 April 2024, 'Cycle of Catechesis: Vices and Virtues 13', <www.vatican.va/content/francesco/en/audiences/2024/documents/20240403-udienza-generale.html#:~:text=Justice%20is%20a%20virtue%20for,justice%2%E2%80%A6>. Accessed 9 December 2024.

honesty'. Seen in these terms, that is, as a complex of virtues, justice has scope; it has range, and it has layers. However, I think the list is incomplete without 'forgiveness'.

Forgiveness is a virtue that is highlighted in that most ubiquitous of liturgical expressions, the Lord's Prayer: 'Forgive us our sins as we forgive those who sin against us'. Clearly, we are not forgiven unless we forgive. This virtue underpins our liturgical practice. It is part of the communion rite: We do not come to the table until we have pledged to forgive and until we have offered the sign of peace to those around us.

I would suggest that in all our liturgical celebrations we are called to be benevolent, respectful, grateful, affable, honest and forgiving. Of course, we do not always manage to live up to these ideals. Neither did some of the earliest Christians, at least according to St Paul in First Corinthians (11:20–22). In scathing terms, Paul criticised the Corinthian Christians for their snobbishness while sharing the Lord's Supper, accusing them of showing contempt for the church and humiliating the needy.

If contemporary commentators such as Elizabeth Harrington are still compelled to remind us to be concerned about Eucharist and justice, then that means we keep making the same mistakes generation after generation. This is why we, the people of God, need to persevere in our efforts to balance the glorious ideals of our liturgical practices with the concrete realities related to justice in the world.

Glory

Glory is a confusing concept and until recently I did not have a handle on it at all. Some time ago, I was in my parish church singing the Gloria with the congregation when I had a lightbulb moment: After a lifetime of singing the Gloria, I had no idea what it really meant. I asked myself two questions: What is glory anyway? What does it mean to give glory to God? I felt compelled to investigate these knotty issues.

Glory in the Gospel of John

After months of trawling though a myriad of sources, I was drawn back, time and again, in the direction of John's gospel. Johannine scholar Dorothy Lee offers a few ideas in her book *Transfiguration*.[3] Of course, the story of the transfiguration is only recorded in the synoptic gospels, nonetheless Lee claims that the gospel of John is a transfiguration narrative. She writes that transfiguration symbols

> have their background in Old Testament imagery that is common to the New Testament writers. However, where there is a congruence of symbols, especially those associated with light, glory and revelation, we may detect echoes, if not actual knowledge of the transfiguration story.[4]

I am not going to make an argument about the transfiguration story, but Lee's alignment of 'light, glory and revelation' is interesting. I think that light and revelation are manifestations of God's glory in the world. If you join the light and revelation together you get 'enlightenment', and this is one useful way to refer to the manifestation of God's glory.

I chose a few stories from scripture to test out this idea a little. First, the story from Exodus in which God's self-revelation emerged from a blazing bush: 'I am who I am' (Exod 3:14). So, I am taking these elements, that is, the presence of God (revelation) in the flaming bush (light), as an expression of the glory of God. Second, in the story of Jesus' baptism,[5] the heavens were torn apart and the Spirit descended like a dove, and God's voice identified Jesus as the Beloved. This is the epitome of what might be called 'enlightenment' for the witnesses. And third is the transfiguration itself.[6] Here light and darkness are used as symbols of knowing and unknowing in a paradoxical way: the bedazzling brightness of the figure of Jesus befuddled the disciples, but then, out of the overshadowing cloud, God's voice is heard. This is enlightenment wrapped in mystery.

From these stories, it is clear, that God's glory is not confined to the heavenly realm but evident in the life of the world. Further, these biblical manifestations might have happened long ago, but they did not take place in a vacuum: God's glory was revealed in the real world and in the flow of life. There are several common elements in these stories, but perhaps the most visceral is the felt presence of God for those who witnessed the events.

---

3. Dorothy A Lee, *Transfiguration* (London: Continuum, 2004).
4. Lee, *Transfiguration*, 100.
5. Matt 3:14–17, Mk 1:9–11, Lk 3:21–22
6. Matt 17:1–8, Mk 9:2–13, Lk 9:28–36; see also 2 Pet 1:16–19.

Everyday Glory

Turning to the present, I want to make some claims about how the glory of God can be experienced in everyday life. It is a given that God is always with us, in every moment and in every place. Consequently, we have any number of opportunities to experience enlightenment every day in even the most ordinary events of our lives: when we see the sun rise, when we hear the gurgling laughter of a baby, when we witness one person going out of their way to show kindness to another. These can all be life-giving experiences of God's presence in the world, but to notice them we need eyes to see and ears to hear (Matt 13:16). Otherwise, this multitude of opportunities for enlightenment will pass us by unnoticed.

What about negative experiences such as sickness and devastating loss? In those instances, when heart calls out to heart, God's presence can also be experienced. But is this also glory? Why not? It is not so much the experience itself that is God's glory, but the felt presence of God in that situation. Our encounter with God is a separate reality from the mediating experience itself, and yet the two cannot be separated. It does not matter if the experience is significant or minor, pleasurable or disagreeable, comforting or disturbing—anything can be a catalyst for encountering God's glory.

If I am right, then glory is nothing special. In fact, it is the most common element in the world—more common than the oxygen we breathe—and yet it is precious. God's glory is ever present in creation, but it is only evident to us and effective as enlightenment, if we are attentive to the presence of God in the flow of life: if we have eyes to see and ears to hear.

Dorothy Lee says that John's gospel uses glory 'in its Old Testament sense to signify the radiant presence of God with Israel, a presence that is both loving and life-giving'.[7] Lee also claims that John's use of 'glory is profoundly christological: In his flesh Jesus is the revelation of divine glory because the same radiance—the majestic yet intimate presence that is a major characteristic of the transfiguration—is revealed in him'.[8] So Jesus is the embodiment of glory.

---

7. Lee, *Transfiguration*, 103.
8. Lee, *Transfiguration*, 104.

Glory as the Revelation of God's Love

This christological connection leads to my next source. In his final book, *Meditations on Holy Week,* Anthony Kelly writes that '"glory" seems to be one of those basic notions that can never be satisfactory pinned down in precise definition'.[9] However, he does link the notion of glory directly to the person of Jesus: 'the life-giving glory of God . . . will climactically shine forth in the self-giving of Jesus on the Cross' and 'in the light of that final disclosure, the life and deeds of the Son would be interpreted as the unveiling of the glory of God'.[10]

Kelly follows Johannine scholar Frank Moloney here. Moloney gives a compelling definition of glory: 'What Jesus reveals on the Cross is in fact the revelation of God's love . . . and that is called Glory'.[11] For Moloney, love equals glory. Kelly also aligns love and glory with the cross: 'through the Cross of Jesus, the glory of self-giving love, the true form of life everlasting is disclosed . . .' and in 'the realm of glory, love is the decisive life-value, "for God is love" (1 Jn 4:8)'.[12] Moloney identifies glory as 'the visible manifestation [in the world] of the presence of a caring God'.[13] This definition supports the arguments I made above, first, about the way we can experience God's glory in everyday life and second, that glory is a common element in creation.

Both Kelly and Moloney focus on the cross as the proof of God's love: Love and glory become one in the cross. On the other hand, Dorothy Lee includes every aspect of the life of Jesus as the embodiment of 'God's indwelling'.[14] I stand with Lee on this issue. The person of Jesus, his life and mission, death and resurrection are all inclusive in the expression of God's glory. Further, I have long held that the Cross is not a complete symbol by itself.

This notion was in my mind as I designed the logo for the Australian Academy of Liturgy Conference 2025 (pictured).

---

9. Anthony Kelly, *Meditations on Holy Week* (Adelaide: ATF Press, 2023), 89.
10. Kelly, *Meditations*, 90–91.
11. Frank Moloney, 'The Gospel of John: Joy Made Complete', Session 9: John 13–17: The Glory of Love (Broken Bay Bible Conference, Caroline Chisholm Centre, Pennant Hills, 13 September 2014), <www.youtube.com/watch?v=2hUkv1-77wc>. Accessed 5 August 2025.
12. Kelly, *Meditations*, 92.
13. Moloney, 'The Gospel of John'.
14. Lee, *Transfiguration*, 105.

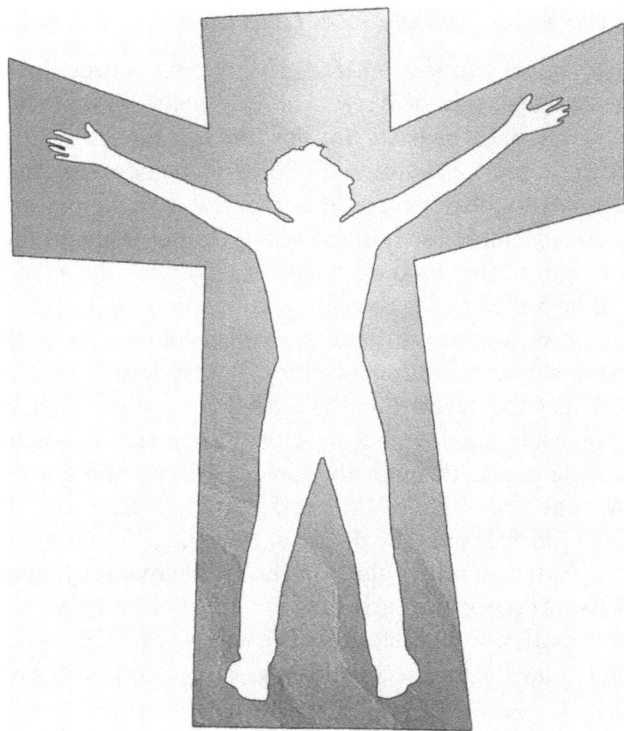

The theme of the conference was 'Justice at the Heart of the Liturgy'. I included the figure of Jesus, not as a corpse in a crucifixion, but as a living person whose words and deeds, not just his death, are paramount.

Heaven and earth are drawn together in the whole story of Jesus: the incarnation, the mission, the death, the resurrection. However, one significant element is missing in my logic, and that is the sending of the Holy Spirit. Of course, no single image tells the whole story. Nonetheless, the image points in the direction of the conjunction of glory and justice in the expression and embodiment of God's love in the world.

Glory and Justice

Garry Deverell links love and justice in a particular way in his book *Gondwana Theology*. He writes, 'For Christians . . . love has a content'. Deverell is referring specifically to justice issues of the First Nations peoples in Australia, adding that 'For First Peoples . . . the call to love takes a particular shape'.[15]

Deverell points to the story of the Canaanite woman in Matthew (15:21–28), in which the woman is initially ignored by Jesus. Then through her persistence, faith and courage—born out of the desperation of a mother's love—she changes Jesus' mind. Deverell writes, 'Clearly her experience with God has taught her something that Jesus himself had not yet learned: that God's love extends even to those beyond one's own tribe'.[16] If we apply Moloney's definition here—that love equals glory—then it is evident that the glory of God was manifested when love overcame prejudice. Glory and justice were reconciled in the story of the Canaanite woman.

Love has a content and a particular shape because it is not a universal concept; that is, love does not mean the same thing in every place and in every time, and it does not work the same way for everyone. Love also has a context; in Deverell's book the context is the experience of injustice by Indigenous Christians in Australia today.

Considering the particularity of love's content and context, the reconciliation of glory and justice does not happen in some idyllic realm outside of ordinary experience but in the flow of life. It does not happen without effort on our part, as John 15:8 indicates: 'By this my Father is glorified, that you bear much fruit, and so prove to be my disciples'. So, when we care for one another, especially for the disadvantaged—working for justice in the world—our efforts are an expression of God's love and God's glory.

In my local parish, I am a member of the St Vincent de Paul Society. Reaching out to those in need with my fellow Vincentians is one concrete way that I try to link theory and practice—glory and justice—in my own Christian living. I am reminded of Dorothy Lee's alignment of glory, light and revelation. For me, being a Vincentian means being Christ for the world: being enlightened and revelatory in caring for others. I am not patting myself on the back here: This is just a common or garden-variety way of being a disciple.

When we celebrate liturgy as true disciples, having taken up our cross in life and working for justice in the world, then God's

---

15. Garry Worete Deverell, *Gondwana Theology: A Trawloolway Man Reflects on Christian Faith* (Adelaide, SA: ATF Theology, 2024), 60.
16. Deverell, *Gondwana Theology,* 61.

glory is manifested in us. This reminds me of the famous saying of St Irenaeus: 'The glory of God is a human being fully alive'.[17] In his original context, Irenaeus was referring to Jesus as the exemplar of humanity; nonetheless, the saying can be applied to us too. I take it to mean living life to the full and that means being enlightened, which in turn means being attentive to the revelation of God's love in everyday life and paying it forward.

In her article 'Glorifying the Lord by Your Life',[18] Judy Foster juxtaposed the writings of St John Chrysostom with a contemporary sculpture *Homeless Jesus* by Canadian artist Timothy Schmaltz (pictured).

Homeless Jesus by Timothy Schmaltz, bronze sculpture. Photo by MJ Crocker. Used with permission of the artist.

Schmaltz's life-size bronze sculpture has been reproduced many times around the world, and this iteration was installed in the forecourt of the Sacred Heart Cathedral in Townsville in 2017. The marks of the crucifixion can be seen on the feet of the figure, so this is clearly Jesus. Foster writes that, over the years, she had often seen people sitting beside the figure and interacting with it.[19] The sculpture is a reflection on the Last Judgment described by Jesus in Matthew's gospel. One of

---

17. Irenaeus of Lyons, *Adversus haereses*, 4.20.7.
18. Judith Foster, 'Glorify the Lord by Your Life', in *The Art of Liturgical Celebration*, edited by Clare Schwantes (Brisbane: Liturgy Brisbane, 2024), 305–317.
19. Judith Foster, 'Glorify the Lord', 307.

the key messages here is 'as you did it to one of the least of these, you did it to me' (Matt 25:34–40).

Foster is interested in Chrysostom's alignment of Eucharist and justice in his commentary on Mathew 25: 'If you wish to honour Christ's body, then do not neglect him when he is naked. Do not honour him here [in the church] with silken garments while neglecting him outside as he perishes from the cold and from a lack of clothing'. Chrysostom adds, 'He who said, "this is my body", also said, "You saw me hungry and did not feed me". Spend your wealth on the poor since God has no need of golden vessels but of golden souls'.[20]

Foster gives Chrysostom's notion of 'golden souls' a contemporary application:

> Golden souls are those who understand their baptismal gift of justice as well as the relationship of the whole Body of Christ, beyond a narrow theology of the eucharistic species. Christ is not only on the altar and in the tabernacle. Christ is wrapped up in an old blanket on the bench outside the church.[21]

The title of Foster's article is a quote from one of the dismissals from the Roman Missal: 'Go in peace, glorifying the Lord by your life'.[22] So the author imagines that we take our eucharistic experience with us when we leave the church and pay it forward. And this is, I think, what we are saying when we sing the Gloria.

The Gloria

My initial confusion about the meaning of the Gloria was focused mainly on the first line: 'Glory to God in the highest'. Obviously, this is a reference to Luke's infancy narrative when the heavenly hosts appeared to the shepherds: The angels were announcing the birth of Jesus and praising God.[23] That is the immediate reference, but there is something else going on when we sing this phrase today: We are

---

20. John Chrysostom, *Homily 50 on Matthew*, <https://www.newadvent.org/fathers/200150.htm>. Accessed 19 December 2024.
21. Foster, 'Glorify the Lord by Your Life', 316.
22. *The Roman Missal*, 'The Concluding Rites', third edition (Catholic Truth Society, 2010), 708.
23. Lk 2:14

singing about ourselves. We are proclaiming ourselves to be the embodiment of God's glory on earth and, therefore, the embodiment of God's love in the world.

This is a huge claim to make, because it means that we are boasting that we are human beings fully alive, golden souls, living enlightened lives, revealing God's self-giving love in our particular context, with the shape and content of our own experience and working for justice in the world. But—and this is a big but—can we honestly sing 'Glory to God in the highest' knowing that all of this is what we are claiming?

Of course, these ideals are aspirational at best and maybe that is enough, as long as we keep trying to live up to them by caring for our neighbour. If so, then our liturgical expressions will shape the way we understand who God is, which in turn will shape the way we live our lives. Then also, our liturgies will reflect our values: benevolence, respectfulness, gratitude, affability, honesty and forgiveness. And in the brief moments when we can achieve such an ideal state, glory and justice will be reconciled across liturgy and life.

Academy Reports

President's Report

The AAL Committee (formerly the Council) has been meeting monthly in the latter part of 2025. We are delighted that Adam Couchman has assumed the role of treasurer and has stepped into the role with great gusto. Renewal of the annual subscription has now been completed. Thank you to both Adam and Jason McFarland (our former treasurer) for doing this.

State convenors will be following up with any annual memberships that remain unpaid from previous years. Members who may be behind are asked to check previous yearly renewals. Members are also reminded of their responsibility to inform the state convenor or executive of postal address changes.

The Committee has recently discussed two papers prepared by Kieran Crichton, first on the AAL website renewal and secondly on the AAL conferences. The latter has been discussed at several state chapter gatherings, and we thank members for their responses.

The Committee feel that it would be good to return to our previous practice of gathering for the AAL national conference on the year that Societas Liturgica does not meet for its international conference. Both groups met in 2025, and some members who usually attend both had to make a choice about their attendance at one or the other.

The good news is that members of the New South Wales chapter have offered to host the next national conference in Sydney on the last week of September 2026. They are undertaking site visits and developing proposals for the Committee by the end of the year. Many thanks to the New South Wales chapter members. All members will have received a 'date claimer' by the end of 2025 for the 2026 conference. Members are invited to consider contributing short papers for the next conference.

Thanks as always to Bryan Cones and the editorial team of this journal. This year has been a rich one for papers. Every encouragement is once again given to all members to submit an article to Bryan or to initiate a proposal for a future article with him.

John Fitz-Herbert, President
johnfrancisfitzherbert@gmail.com

Victoria Chapter Report

The Victoria Chapter met in September 2025 for the primary purpose of appointing a new Chapter Convenor. Kieran Crichton had completed eight years in the role and is now a member of the National AAL Committee. Kieran had undertaken some administration processes to aid the chapter going forward, shifting from using personal contact details when dealing with chapter business to the chapter's new email address: liturgy.victoria@gmail.com.

People were asked to nominate someone and the resultant discussion led to the appointment of myself, Peter Sheehan, as the new Chapter Convenor beginning in 2025. I have been a member of the AAL for approximately ten years, joining at the end of 2015 after completing a Master of Arts in Theology with units in liturgy and liturgical music. Between 2016 and 2019 I completed a Bachelor of Music majoring in singing. I left Catholic Church circles for approximately twenty years, and was involved in worship ministry, worship leadership and production teams in Anglican, Baptist, Churches of Christ and various Pentecostal church groups. I then became a 'revert' and returned to the Catholic Church in 2007.

Next month, the Australian Catholic Youth Festival (ACYF) is being held in Melbourne from 30 November to 2 December. The ACYF is a three-day festival bringing together thousands of young people from across Australia. The festival will include opportunities for engagement with other young people, school and youth groups, bishops, musicians and speakers, including Fr Rob Galea and Cardinal Mykola Bychok. Each day will include the opportunity to engage in a wide range of activities including prayer, Mass, workshops, talks, live concerts, games, justice issues and an interactive expo.

Peter Sheehan, Victoria Chapter Convenor
kefa.music@icloud.com

Queensland Chapter Report

The Queensland chapter have continued to meet every two months during 2025. We have a core group of twenty members across the state who are dedicated to this time together. Our core group remains ecumenical, with the lively participation of members from respective churches. Due to recent technical difficulties at our meeting venue, we have held the last several meetings on Zoom only. At our November meeting we agreed to explore meeting in 2026 at St Francis' College (Anglican) in Milton, both in person and on Zoom.

At each meeting we pray together and share liturgical events and matters from our churches. This often has a local feel to it which builds local ecumenical awareness. At recent meetings we have discussed the range of articles in the most recent issue of the journal and acknowledged the twentieth anniversary of *Uniting in Worship 2*. We also discussed the document on future AAL conferences prepared by AAL Vice President Kieran Crichton. We appreciated Kieran inviting us to think forward on our conferences.

We are looking forward to gathering at the end of this year over a meal and drinks.

John Fitz-Herbert, Queensland Chapter Convenor
johnfrancisfitzherbert@gmail.com

Western Australian Chapter Report

Our chapter currently has eleven members, and we are meeting via Zoom so that we can gather in our diversity. At our most recent meeting in the beginning of November, various members had travelled for liturgical reasons. Two of us were in Assisi in May for the ecumenical meeting regarding the Feast/Season of Creation and were able to offer a summary of ideas and directions. Angela McCarthy has been appointed as a consultant to the Bishops' Commission for Liturgy and proposed a letter of information for the commission, as the proposal from the Assisi movement had been rejected by the Australian bishops. The long-lasting effect of this establishment of a liturgical feast is more likely to be the ecumenical connection rather than the crisis of climate change.

Three of our members were present at the Adelaide conference in October for the Australian Pastoral Musicians Network and National Liturgical Council. It was a very well attended conference and the keynote speakers from the USA, Fr Ricky Manalo and Rita Ferrone, offered wonderful material. Manolo spoke of our hybrid identity in liturgy and life, and all three attendees were affected by his presentation.

One of our members had only recently returned from a pilgrimage to Rome for the Jubilee Year and recounted his experience, followed by a holiday in France and Scotland. Another member is the Dean of St George's Cathedral in Perth, and he gave us an insight into his role.

We welcome new members and look forward to meeting again in late January or early February.

Angela McCarthy, Western Australia Chapter Convenor
drpelican53@gmail.com

South Australia Chapter Report

The South Australia Chapter is delighted to welcome Rev Richard Telfer as a new member, and to welcome Rev Geoff Johnston back after his sojourn in placements in other places. At the final meeting of the chapter on 28 October, we welcomed Henry Novello as a guest. We have been reading his book, *Setting our Hearts upon the Deep: Acknowledging Lament in Christian Life, Worship and Thought* (Pickwick Publications, 2023). After teaching systematic theology at the University of Notre Dame (Fremantle), he is currently honorary research fellow in the School of Humanities at Flinders University.

Alison Whish, South Australia Chapter Convenor
Alisonwhish@outlook.com

New South Wales Chapter Report

The New South Wales Chapter has met regularly this year at Golden Grove Centre, Newtown in February, June and September. Many members also attended the National Conference in Brisbane in January. At our February meeting we discussed the conference and the papers presented, our learnings and thoughts on gathering as a national body. In June, we discussed the opening keynote address by Rowan Williams at a conference in Rome, *Nicaea 2025: Context, Event and Reception*. We viewed his presentation, 'Restoring the Image: Theological Anthropology and the Creed of Nicaea', via YouTube, and so we were able to see and hear Williams.

In September our gathering reflected on the upcoming presentation by chapter members Elizabeth Murray, SGS and Elizabeth Brennan, SGS titled, 'Introducing the Daily Prayer of the Church to Your Parish'. This presentation is to be made at the Pilgrims of Hope conference in October. We also heard from four members who attended the *Societas Liturgica* Congress earlier in the month in Paris. At the October online meeting we heard from chapter member Chris Ohlsen, who presented his master's thesis, 'The Roman Catholic Funeral: Celebrating the Mystery of Life in Christ'. We also discussed the possibility of Sydney hosting the next national conference of the academy and elected the state convenor.

It has been a productive and energetic year for the chapter with these regular gatherings, attendance at conferences, and welcoming new members. This energy level is set to continue in 2026 with the national conference.

David Nelson, New South Wales Chapter Convenor
liturgy.cathedral@cdob.org.au

Book Reviews

What Is Happening to Religion in Australia? Understanding the Trends
by Philip Hughes
Coventry Press, 2025, 157 pages

Reviewed by Stephen Burns, Victoria

This book hardly mentions liturgy or worship, so its primary connection with this journal is by way of shared emphasis on Australia in both the book's and the journal's title, and via the journal's intent 'to further the study of liturgy at a scholarly level and to comment and provide information concerning liturgical matters with special reference to Australia' and to 'focus on Australia and the work of Australian scholars...' (to quote twice from the AJL's very first issue). Philip Hughes' book is certainly of help with 'focus on Australia', though it will be up to his readers to keep thinking about what we learn from it in relation to 'liturgical matters'.

The author, long associated with the Christian Research Association, and with posts before retirement at Harvest Bible College and AlphaCrucis, is himself a Uniting (and former Baptist) minister. He begins personally with stories of three church communities he served as minister—his way of inviting readers into the trends he then sketches on a large canvas. In part, this book tells us things we already know, about an 'overall scene... of declining church attendance' (xvi). But it does this with both force and grace, and it adds insights to what at least I already knew, so that may also be true for others.

The bare facts are potent: In 1921 97 percent of Australians identified as Christian, but by 2021 only 44 percent did (7). This is slightly more across the general population than among Aboriginal and Torres Strait Islanders (41 percent Christian, 9). Though decline across the whole began with the Baby Boomer generation, the recent rate of dropout is dizzying, with only 10 percent of the 2021 population attending church regularly (with 'regularly' meaning once or more monthly). From 2011 to 2021 churches together declined 15 percent, although were it not for immigration that number would be more than 20 percent (79). Some denominations have declined faster than others: those who welcome immigrants the least—though it is immigrants who are '"saving" the churches' (78)—and 'progressive' churches, which might think they are trendy but still tend to be slow at catching up with what the general population thinks.

Pentecostals along with immigrants (associated with whatever denomination) attend more than others (82, 98). But reactions against the authoritarian style of leadership which can mark some Pentecostal contexts is noted in relation to the observation that Pentecostalism is in fact in decline (65, 97). Pentecostals, though, do have the second largest group of regular attenders, after Catholics, followed by Anglicans, then Baptists. Both Anglicans (once second, but now with just 10 percent of the population) and Uniting (once third, but now with only 4 percent) are among the 'progressives'—but not necessarily given the conservatism of some Australian Anglicans. In any case, churches with 'conservative' teaching—for example, Roman Catholic prohibitions against artificial birth control—can expect to be widely ignored, evidenced in that Catholic families are now smaller than Protestant ones. Catholics do, though, tend to identify with their church longer after they stop attending than their Protestant peers.

All churches are becoming more conservative, as conservative types have stayed while many more progressive members have given up. And even currently thriving ethnic-minority majority communities can expect to decline, as the next generation of immigrant families acclimatise to an Australian cultural milieu with more social welfare and less pro-traditional families (around heterosexual couples, supported by marriage) than the environments from which their elders came. Prospects for migrant Christian groups are juxtaposed with those belonging to other great faiths (Sikhism is burgeoning, 14), all of which are also dependent on immigration for much of whatever growth they have seen.

Numbers and what they suggest about trends in church attendance are set in a wider scope by the book's detailing of changes in Australians' personal and social mores, along with medical and technological 'advances' (disease eradication is mentioned, but not evermore deadly weapons). Unsurprisingly for several decades, sex and gender have so often been matters in the middle of the dissonance between churches and wider society: '[N]owhere is conflict so strong as in relation to sexuality' (65).

A newer layer of deep trouble has also been added by the scandal of abuse in ecclesial contexts, and this has upturned any claim to moral authority the churches may have once thought they had. Churches have been 'revealed as wrongdoers' (68) and the offense they have caused and their 'fail[ure] at contemporary moral standards' (70) evokes 'anger' (74, 88–9). This strand on anger is one of the compelling aspects of this book. I was also struck by Hughes's attention to differences between values that tend to be held by people in the 'business class' vis-a-vis the 'knowledge class' (in education and caring professions), and how the latter have remained more committed to churches while the loss of the former has contributed to decline. Another insightful sub-strand is about how while some of the 'knowledge class' have stayed with church, this class also makes up the heft of those who now see themselves as 'spiritual but not religious', valuing care but no longer the church's beliefs, and who are 'unlikely to return to church' (113).

The last two chapters of the book explore different kinds of ways people now make 'meaning', and how the churches might find ways to engage them. One of the key clues is that churches must not 'persist' in causing offence (138). Another relates to being much better all round for children, given current patterns suggesting that most adults who attend did so as children themselves. Churches will have to organise their whole life to prioritise ministry to children. The attitude will have to be—in relation to children and in everything else—one of 'serving others rather than trying to lord it over' (139) and 'reaffirm[ing] that [churches'] priority is service, not taking control' (140), searching for ways through such service to put themselves in the centre of the wider community.

This means, in turn, *not* 'focus[ing] more on their inner life than on justice and wellbeing in the wider society' (137) and certainly not 'merging' (amalgamating/uniting) to sustain their inward-focused activities, for 'merging leads to smaller congregations and thus to faster decline' (130). Another of the clues is small groups, where small churches might at their best, to allow for opportunities to join things other than 'Sunday services [which] attract some but not others' (134). Such small groups may be for Bible study and/or prayer, but also 'mission' and 'action' (131). These small groups turn out to be important even in large churches, though large ones can also provide as part of their appeal opportunity for 'anonymity' which is attractive to those unlikely to be drawn to small groups and who actively choose the 'fringe' (131), which is harder to do in small churches.

Hughes's few references to liturgy include—in discussion of whether stressing denominational or other distinctiveness leads to growth—the point that some might come because they enjoy it (the music or preaching), but this is usually not enough to keep people over time. Liturgy also gets a mention in relation to the interesting observation that Protestant worship often presumes 'knowledge class' values of reading and joining responsive liturgies, whereas Catholic Mass might not put such stress on knowledge class mores, and hence draws a wider spectrum of people. Mass is mentioned again when noting that it being celebrated in many languages gestures welcome to immigrants. Welcome is also intended by the casual ('business') style of leaders' dress favoured by some 'conservative' churches, along with screens and contemporary music in worship—and there is a repeated mention of 'music and speakers' (96, 131), not 'preachers'—a curious reference, perhaps, in the shade of other observations that teaching (in preaching?) is often ignored.

Notably, not only is liturgy or worship barely mentioned, neither are ministers. They are cited in relation to abuse of course, but otherwise rare references are in the context of talk of lay leadership of services (including in some contexts, sacraments—as presiders as in some traditions, or at communion from 'reserved sacrament' or 'eucharistic adoration' in others, or what, we do not learn). Ministers might perhaps be part of teams (a 'team minister') responsible for 'resourcing' the team. But 'the reality is that many ministers will oversee declining churches' (128)—and perhaps, if Gary Bouma is right, 'the era of religious professionals is at an end' (132).

So not offending (however that might best be navigated), putting children first, looking and going outward, and having different things to join in as well as not chasing the fringe-dwellers are some of the challenges from this book in terms of working its insights through as 'liturgical matters' (to invoke again this journal's purpose). Questions abound: What is preaching for in the culture we inhabit? And if 'regular' attendance may be just once a month, what to make of lectionary patterns which presume continuities, apart from some sense of seasons? On the latter might anything be made, as Hughes suggests it might, of engaging people more in what they already 'celebrate' in 'civic religion': Valentine's Day, Easter appeals for hospitals and such like, Anzac memories, mother's and father's days—more challenge to only fragilely established liturgical seasons, out of sync with their origins in relation to northern equinoxes and solstices?

Our most basic questions must be to do with how churches do or might yet conceive worship as *outward-focused* activity, and then about *what else* they do alongside worship. Without good answers to these questions, it seems that all is lost. Given Hughes's emphasis on the churches' need to prioritise outgoing *service* to the communities in which they are set, rather than focus internally on their dwindling congregations, much thinking is needed in this journal and elsewhere about if and how 'liturgy' might be retrieved in its basic meaning as '*public* service'.

Mystery Manifest: The Triune God, Figuratively Speaking
by Gail Ramshaw
Fortress Press, 2025, 234 pages

Reviewed by Annie Brophy, Victoria

Lutheran scholar Gail Ramshaw has dedicated her 'life's work' (15) to the task of finding liturgical language for God. She has never shied away from the feminist commitments that motivate her work and much of her effort has focused on finding language that reaches beyond gender. Even so, a parallel commitment has been a dedication to finding language that expresses something of the mystery of God, even as it acknowledges the limits of that language's capacity to name the ineffable and give expression to the numinous. Given that Ramshaw has already written so extensively over decades on this topic, it would be easy to assume that there is 'nothing new under the sun' in this, her latest book. While it is indeed a valuable addition to the Ramshaw canon—one which represents her 'mature thinking on this complex issue' (9)—far from being just a rehash of earlier work, this book is a rich resource for both public and private prayer in its own right

Mystery Manifest is a thoughtfully organised and cogently structured book which serves to systematise Ramshaw's thinking and enhances the possibilities the book presents for use as a navigable reference—and with 'over 250 figures of speech' (9) included, that is a significant benefit. The comprehensive index at the end of the book is also crucial in this regard. The first two chapters form the foundation for succeeding chapters, with the first chapter containing echoes of the author's previous work, engaging with language at the intersection of mystery, fact, truth, and linguistics, and setting the groundwork and parameters for what follows. It delves into the 'Why and Where' of the need to find language to and about God, as well as how that pursuit fits into a culture that needs and relies on 'accurate speech' (14) to function well and effectively.

The second chapter is a case study of a 'somewhat rare' way of speaking about God—God the Fire (41). While most of the figures of speech referenced in this book are accompanied by a relatively short 'explanatory comment' or 'interpretive reflection', this exploration of God the Fire is illustrative of the breadth and depth of enquiry employed in Ramshaw's lifelong engagement with the question: 'What does this mean?' (9). She comes at this question from numerous angles and through this extended example, invites the reader to join her in the quest.

Following from this, subsequent chapters contain the lists of figures of speech for God, Jesus, Holy Spirit and the Trinity respectively. In each chapter the figures of speech are typically grouped alphabetically in related clusters. For example, those related to figures of speech for God in Chapter 3, are arranged around the following categories: objective figures of speech in Psalm 18 (57); anthropomorphic figures of speech in Psalm 18 (60); objective figures of speech from throughout the Bible (63); anthropomorphic figures of speech from throughout the Bible (67); objective figures of speech from Christians past and present (76); and anthropomorphic figures of speech from Christians past and present (80). The logic behind the author's organisation of these categories is obvious: She employs a clear typology distinguishing *objective* from *anthropomorphic* figures of speech, applied across three contexts—Psalm 18, the wider biblical corpus, and Christian tradition. The subsequent chapters are similarly well organised, although along different yet appropriate lines of logic and connection.

There are several things which stand out about this book, and a brief mention of those here may be helpful for people to assess the book's usefulness to their context and particular interests. The first is Ramshaw's obvious commitment to education around language, theology, and gender. She frames the lists of figures of speech in such a way as to set them in conversation with broader theological issues and questions both historical and current. An example of the former, for example is her overview of Arianism under the heading 'Some Second Person Issues to Consider' (116) in her chapter on language for and about Jesus.

Also notable is that Ramshaw is unafraid to engage with the challenging, controversial, or downright strange. For example, she presses into questions such as: At what point does Christian license become permission for antisemitism (50)? Is it 'problematic' to refer to the first testament as the 'Old Testament' (49)? She challenges the literalisation of parables (27), as well as the traditionally mute acceptance of references to female bodies and its reproductive features while 'in neither the Scriptures nor the tradition is found comparable male imagery of bodily reproduction' (70).

The diversity of figures of speech Ramshaw engages with shows just how broad the variety of sources are that she has mined for them. From the obvious biblical sources to church fathers to contemporary scholars as well as poets, hymnwriters and artists throughout the centuries, there is a sense in which Ramshaw has left no stone unturned in her quest to find language for God, but that she is also open to and expecting to find more.

There is a thread of joy running through this book. Ramshaw's at times wry observations and questions convey a feeling that she enjoyed researching and writing it as much as she anticipates her possible readers will. While she is quite firm about the direction of the conversation, there is no question that this book is framed as conversation and invitation. That this is so is clear in her clever use of questions throughout the book (a feature which means this book would also lend itself for use in a liturgically interested discussion group). These questions are sometimes provocative, sometimes wry, and sometimes entirely rhetorical—or perhaps inserted as a means for the reader to pause, to assimilate the information and to ask their own questions about the language they use for God. The questions are an invitation to consider how we really feel about particular figures of speech, then to interrogate, perhaps, why we feel the way we do. Does the figure of speech somehow challenge our own safe metaphors and images? Have we perhaps turned a figure of speech into an idol? The questions also invite the reader to delve deeper and engage with the figures of speech more closely (in the manner of the God the Fire chapter) and to draw our own conclusions as to their aptness. While Ramshaw's voice is firm and sure, she challenges but is never prescriptive or dogmatic.

Ramshaw is clear at the outset what the parameters and limits of this book are: It does not claim to be an 'exhaustive' list of language for God and is therefore necessarily focussed on 'is' nouns, words that are set parallel to 'God' (13). Even so, this is a rich and varied contribution to the lexicon of language for God.

AJL Addresses

AJL addresses
Manuscripts for publication to: The Editor, AJL
Email: bmcones@gmail.com
Books for review should be sent to: The Book Review Editor, AJL
Email: michellejeastwood@gmail.com

Authors preparing manuscripts are requested to follow the Chicago Manual of Style, 17th edition, for footnotes, which is available at many online locations. AJL does not use the Harvard or author-date system. Manuscripts should be free of formatting related to citation programs, such as EndNote, and should not contain external hyperlinks or other internal links. Texts which insufficiently adhere to these will be returned for correction.

Peer-reviewed research articles should not normally exceed 5,000 words in length. Other essays may range between 1,500 and 3,000 words. Book reviews may range between 500 words for a short (one-page) review; longer reviews may extend to 1,000 words. Decisions regarding publication are made in consultation with editorial panel and at the discretion of the editor.

Articles may be submitted by an attachment to an email. Photographs must be of sufficient size (greater than 1 MB) and definition to print in black and white; photo files should be provided separately from the text, preferably in JPEG format. A photo of the author, a short biographical statement, and an abstract are required. Only articles not previously published and not under consideration for publication elsewhere will be accepted. All articles submitted will be reviewed by the AJL editorial panel or other reviewers with appropriate expertise.

The Australian Journal of Liturgy is listed in the Register of Refereed Journals published by the Department of Education, Science and Training (DEST), Canberra.

Copyright © Australian Academy of Liturgy

ISSN 1030-617X The Australian Journal of Liturgy should be abbreviated as AJL.

Subscription inquiries to:
The Secretary
c/o Dr Jenny Close
Australian Academy of Liturgy
liturgy.australia@gmail.com

AAL membership:

> $53 Membership full rate (Australia & NZ); $58 Membership (other countries)
> $58 Membership full rate (couple)
> $33 Membership (retired); $38 Membership full rate (retired couple)

AJL subscription:

> $38 Subscription in Australia
> $48 Overseas subscription
> $15 plus postage for additional copies

Advertising is accepted: $20 per half page.

www.ingramcontent.com/pod-product-compliance
Lightning Source LLC
Chambersburg PA
CBHW020904050326
40664CB00005B/246